INSTANT AUTHENTIC SELF CONFIDENCE

Discover The 19 Cognitive & Behavioral Patterns
That Create Immediate Confidence & Self-Esteem

Copyright © 2023 by LearnWell Books.

All rights reserved. No part of this publication may be reproduced, distributed, or transmitted in any form or by any means, including photocopying, recording, or other electronic or mechanical methods, without the prior written permission of the publisher, except in the case of brief quotations embodied in critical reviews and certain other noncommercial uses permitted by copyright law.

References to historical events, real people, or real places are often fictitious. In such cases, the names, characters, and places are products of the author's imagination. We do this where it's important to protect the privacy of people, places, and things.

689 Burke Rd
Camberwell Victoria 3124
Australia

www.LearnWellBooks.com

We're led by God. Our business is also committed to supporting kids' charities. At the time of printing, we have donated well over $100,000 to enable mentoring services for underprivileged children. By choosing our books, you are helping children who desperately need it. Thank you.

**This is really important.
It's a sincere thank you.**

My name is Wayne, the founder of LearnWell.

My Dad put a book in my hands when I was 13. It was written by Zig Ziglar and it changed the course of my life. Since then, it's been books that have helped me get over breakups, learn how to be a good friend, study the lives of good people and books have been the source of my persistence through some pretty challenging times.

My purpose is now to return the favor. To create books that might be the turning point in the lives of people around the world, just like they've been for me. It's enough to almost bring me to tears to think of you holding this book, seeking information and wisdom from something that I've helped to create. I'm moved in a way that I can't fully explain.

We're a small and 'beyond-enthusiastic' team here at LearnWell. We're writers, editors, researchers, designers, formatters (oh … and a bookkeeper!) who take your decision to learn with us incredibly seriously. We consider it a privilege to be part of your learning journey. Thank you for allowing us to join you.

If there's anything we did really well, anything we messed up, or anything AT ALL that we could do better, would you please write to us and tell us (like, right now!) We would love to hear from you!

readers@learnwellbooks.com

We're sending you our thanks, our love and our very best wishes.

Wayne
and the team at LearnWell Books.

WELCOME TO OUR COMMUNITY

"It's like a private online book club"

 Imagine if you could actually meet and talk with other readers of this book and share your experiences.

 Imagine if you could chat with the author or join them on a live Q&A!

 Imagine getting access to the author's notes and other exclusive, unpublished material.

You can do all of that and a lot more in the LearnWell Online Community!!

→ Download your **Workbook**
→ Chat directly with the author!
→ Meet and feel supported by other readers and their experiences.
→ Access additional, exclusive content about this topic and others.
→ Join our live Author Q&A sessions online.
→ Learn faster, make lasting changes, and have 10 times more fun!

All of this is part of our commitment to creating the best learning resources in the world.

Scan the QR code to get FREE access
www.learnwellbooks.com/superstar

To Jack

CONTENTS

Foreword   10

Introduction   12

PART 1: Who Stole Your Confidence?   15

1   Confident – Your Natural State   16

2   What Happened?   24

3   The Confidence Cycles. "Going Up?"   34

PART 2: Powerful New Ways To Think   41

4   But I'm A Fish!   42
      Discover Where You're Already Great

5   It's All Fake   49
      When The Standard Is 'Fake'
      Don't Use That As Your Guide

6   Look At Them   56
      Find Out Who Is The Most Important Person
      To Pay Attention To. (It's Not You)

7   I'm Uncomfortable And I Love It!   61
      How To Slowly Become Bullet-Proof

| 8 | You're Going To Die ... But Not Because Of This | 65 |

    How To Dramatically Increase Your Likelihood Of Success

| 9 | They Don't Like You | 71 |

    How To Find 'Your People'

| 10 | Giggle. A Lot More | 78 |

    The Best Way To Never Be Boring!

| 11 | Who Are You? | 84 |

    The Chance To Create The Best Version Of Yourself

PART 3: Powerful New Things To Do   89

| 12 | Less Talk. More Walk | 90 |

    The Easiest Way To Instantly Become Relevant

| 13 | Do Big Things | 97 |

    How To Get Instant Inspiration

| 14 | Do Little Things | 100 |

    A Guaranteed Method For High Self-Esteem

| 15 | I Accept This. All Of It. Even The Bad Bits | 104 |

    The Fastest Way To Peace

| 16 | Keep Getting Up | 112 |

    The One Ingredient In Life That Ultimately Determines Success

17	Be The Lion And Roar!	118
	How To Use Life-Changing Communication	
18	This Is My Space	124
	How To Set Boundaries That Create Control And Confidence	
19	I Love ME So Much!	129
	Ways Of Showing Love To The Most Lovable Person In The World	
20	Stop! Don't Go There	134
	Gaining Control Of The Most Powerful Tool In Confidence Creation	
21	Chill	140
	How To Create A Mental Environment For Confidence	
22	Pass It On	146
	How To Create A Life Of Escalating Confidence	

PART 4: Your Confidence In Action — 151

Summary — 174

REFERENCES — 179

YOUR WORKBOOK

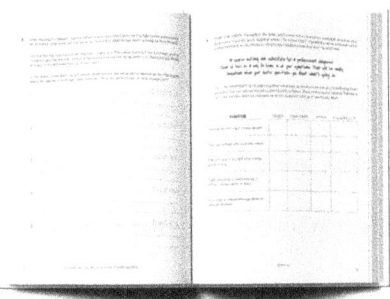

A shocking truth was discovered by a study done in 1987 – **people only remember 10% of what they read!**

That seems so discouraging.

But here's the **GOOD NEWS** – reading is **NEVER** a waste of time. As long as you do **one** important thing ...

The same study (by National Training Laboratories) shows that you will remember 90% of what you read when you **put your new knowledge into action**!

Here at LearnWell, we aim to create **the world's best learning resources**. So, we have included a highly engaging **Workbook** that helps you put your new knowledge into fun, practical action.

So, make sure you download your **FREE Workbook.** You'll find it located inside the **LearnWell Community.** Simply scan the QR code below for access.

Get your Workbook in the LearnWell Community
Scan the QR Code for access or go to:
www.learnwellbooks.com/superstar

FOREWORD

I first started thinking about the importance of self-confidence when I met Jack (that isn't his real name, but I'm sure he'll recognize himself if he's reading this). Jack was great at his job. Intelligent too. Really intelligent, in fact. He was also astonishingly hard-working and willing to regularly work long hours. I joined the same organization and I have to admit – I was initially rather in awe of Jack.

But being successful in your career isn't just about what you do while sitting at your desk. Like almost everything that you do, it's also about how you interact with the world and the people around you. While Jack was great at his day-to-day work in our organization, we also had to give regular public presentations. These would take the form of seminars where we were required to address anything from a couple of dozen to several hundred people. That's something I have never found particularly challenging. Provided I'm given enough time to prepare and I know what I'm talking about, I can reliably deliver a fairly engaging talk no matter how large the audience.

However, standing up in front of a group of strangers seemed to turn Jack into a mumbling zombie. His shoulders would sag, he would look at the floor, his notes, the PowerPoint screen behind him, anywhere but at the people he was supposed to be talking to. He would read out the text of his presentation in a flat monotone voice and then hurry from the stage as quickly as possible. Although Jack had valid and useful points to make, the audience were notably bored: fidgeting, looking at their phones, and even chatting while he droned on.

I started to notice other odd aspects of Jack's behavior. In a one-to-one situation he could communicate well but in meetings, especially large meetings, he tended to say very little. I knew that he had important contributions to make, but he seemed to be unable to articulate them in front of a group. At work-related social events, Jack either didn't attend or spent the evening in a corner chatting to just one person. It gradually became obvious to me that Jack, despite his abilities, would never achieve his full potential because he was hampered by a crippling lack of self-confidence.

I became good friends with Jack but I never spoke to him about this issue although I know that it held him back in his career and I suspect in many other aspects of his life too. That was some time ago and I still regret not talking about this. I subsequently met a number of other people who also suffered from a similar lack of self-confidence. Unlike Jack, some of them were able to dramatically transform their careers and their lives by re-discovering their own innate self-confidence.

That's where this book comes from. It's the outcome of many years of reflection on what self-confidence is, why it matters so much, and how you can rediscover it in yourself. It's a practical, step-by-step guide to how you can make yourself heard, seize opportunities when they present themselves, and live a happier and more fulfilled life. It's about how to become self-confident again.

If you're reading this, Jack, these are all the things I should have said to you…

INTRODUCTION

A lack of self-confidence can be a crippling problem. It can impact every aspect of your life and it can leave you prone to anxiety, depression and low achievement. It can stop you from leading the life that you want and deserve. It affects both men and women to a greater extent than you might imagine:

- It is estimated that up to 85% of the world's population suffer from issues related to low self-esteem and a lack of self-confidence.
- Up to 70% of people admit to lacking confidence at work.
- Up to 60% of people admit to a general lack of confidence[1].

If you are one of the many who suffer from this issue, you will find it difficult to make decisions, to talk to people and to assert your own feelings and needs. You will find it challenging to make friends or have meaningful work or social relationships. You may struggle with negative emotions such as guilt, regret, frustration and shame.

However, a lack-of self-confidence is something you've come to accept over years of conditioning. It's not something you were born with. In fact, you were born with supreme confidence. At one point, you had no concept of fear or self-doubt. You were limitless in your thinking. The great news is that you can restore your innate self-confidence by discovering the practical, easy-to-follow techniques in this book. You will learn robbed you of your self-confidence and what you need to do to regain your right to a confident, fulfilled life.

Introduction

I'm not a doctor or a psychologist but what I do know about self-confidence is that these techniques work. I have spent countless years studying myself and others. I've been witness as hundreds of people have restored their self-confidence applying exactly what I'm sharing with you here. This isn't a mental health textbook: it's a collection of pragmatic advice gathered from the real world and from real people. This is not just a book of ideas: it's about the action <u>you</u> can take to powerfully change <u>your</u> life.

There is nothing mystical here. These techniques are practicable, proven and have been widely used. They <u>will</u> make a difference. You have a choice: you can continue to allow your life to be strangled by a lack of self-confidence. Or you can use this book to change for the better. It's up to you.

This book is structured logically to build your understanding. It begins with the knowledge of how your confidence was eroded. It continues by explaining why we act the way we do in certain circumstances and then provides techniques you can use to change your approach and your state of mind. It will work best if you invest the time to read the whole book. You'll then have all the knowledge you need to take effective action.

However, this book isn't all you'll need. This book is supported by a workbook that includes activities that enrich your learning and help you to see the action you need to take.

 Go to www.learnwellbooks.com/superstar now and download the FREE workbook.

It features exercises, information, advice and much more that will greatly enhance the outcomes you achieve.

INSTANT AUTHENTIC SELF CONFIDENCE

You also have access to the LearnWell Community, which I highly recommend you join along your journey.

Are you tired of having your life restricted by your own lack of confidence? The solution is simple:

- Read this book.
- Download the Workbook and complete the exercises.
- Restore your limitless self-confidence!

PART 1

Who Stole Your Confidence?

CONFIDENT - YOUR NATURAL STATE

The moment you doubt whether you can fly, you cease forever to be able to do it.

– J. M. Barrie, Peter Pan

Have you noticed how some people consistently succeed at whatever they do? They get whatever they chase and they seem to go through life positive, committed, happy, and enthusiastic. Do you know someone like that? Why do you think they're able to do that? It must be because they're smarter than the rest of us, right? Or perhaps harder-working? Or luckier? Or maybe they're just made that way?

The truth is that these people are exactly like the rest of us, but they have one superpower that many people lack: self-confidence. Self-confidence is something that can completely transform your career, your relationships and every other aspect of your life. If you lack self-confidence, you will struggle at almost everything you do. With this superpower you won't only succeed, you'll have fun along the way and the energy you exude will allow others to access their own strength.

When we refer to 'self-confidence', this is what we mean:

When a person expects that their actions are likely to result in the outcomes they desire. The person trusts their own abilities and judgment and believes they can successfully face day-to-day challenges and demands.

Why does having self-confidence matter? Consider the lives of two people, Anne and Pete. Both are in their mid-30s, both are intelligent, married, hard-working and both are keen not just to advance their careers but to make a positive difference to the world. The main difference between them is that while Anne has self-confidence, Pete doesn't.

When a person expects that their actions are likely to result in the outcomes they desire. The person trusts their own abilities and judgment and believes they can successfully face day-to-day challenges and demands.

How does that impact their lives? At work, Anne is always willing to speak up at meetings, putting forward her ideas and offering to work on turning them into reality even when that involves uncertainty or risk. Pete has just as many ideas, but he's very nervous about speaking out in front of a group. He's also afraid of looking stupid or of failing if he does take on something new. He'll even remain silent while he watches colleagues miss important opportunities. Despite the fact that they are equally intelligent, Anne has a reputation for innovation and positivity at work. This serves her well when it's time to think about promotions. Pete, on the other hand, doesn't have such a positive reputation. When he's given a job, he does it competently, but he never seems to have that spark of energy and originality that catches the eye of management. At promotion time, Pete is often passed-over.

Anne has a strong marriage. If she is unhappy about something, she tells her husband about it. That may sometimes cause disagreement, but it also means that they both understand what the other wants and needs. When she's happy, she talks about that too, reinforcing the good times that the two share.

Pete finds himself unable to explain how he feels, even when his wife's behavior makes him feel resentful or angry. His wife believes that the marriage is probably happy, but that's mainly because she has no idea what Pete is really thinking or feeling. That makes her vaguely uneasy and unconsciously unwilling to fully trust her husband.

There is no difference between Anne and Pete in terms of their potential. But the truth is that while Anne seems to enjoy her life, to grasp opportunities and to get what she wants, Pete doesn't achieve any of these things. Anne makes a positive difference to the people around her while Pete seems content to be a passive observer. Anne is also popular both with work colleagues and within her social group. That's not surprising. Most people would rather spend time with someone who has plans and dreams they are willing to share, who is optimistic and whose energy and enthusiasm inspires those around them. Who would you rather spend time with: Anne or Pete?

In my experience, many intelligent, talented, capable people lack self-confidence. When you really think about it, that's odd. If you had met Anne and Pete at the age of five, both would probably have been equally confident. However, different life experiences conspire to undermine self-confidence. That's what the quote at the beginning of this chapter means. Once, you knew how to fly. As you accumulated experiences and created your own interpretations of them,, you lost the ability to fly.

I want you to remember that: if you lack self-confidence now, you didn't always feel that way. That's important. Becoming self-confident isn't about learning a new set of skills or pretending to be something or someone you are not. It's about rediscovering abilities in you that have become dormant. But they're still there, waiting for you to unleash them. You can learn to fly again!

Everyone's soul is dying to express their natural state of calm, centered confidence. Free of anxiety and fear

Pete could be more like Anne if he chose. If he could understand how he had lost his innate self-confidence and what he needed to do to re-awaken it, he could transform his life. You can do the same.

That's what this book is about. It's not a psychological thesis or some mystical approach. It's a wholly practical guide to understanding the techniques you need to re-discover your self-confidence. None of these approaches are complicated though it will take time for them to become embedded as habits. They can be followed by anyone and applied to all aspects of their lives. You simply have to ask yourself a question:

Do you want to find your inner confidence again?

The fact that you're reading this book suggests that you are interested in learning how to regain your self-confidence. Congratulations: recognizing that is a huge step towards transforming your life for the better. Why? Because increased self-confidence will allow you to:

- Look in the mirror every day and see a person you respect and admire.
- Know that your ideas, opinions, and feelings are worthy of attention.
- Set goals, believe in them and take consistent steps toward making them real.
- Create meaningful relationships, communicate strongly, build trust and express your true self.
- Not just have a career but intentionally create one that fulfills you. One that allows you to make a contribution to those around you and to something more than just yourself.

- Operate at the peak of Maslow's Hierarchy – in self-actualization. You'll become the most authentic and empowered version of yourself. Your potential: fully realized.[2]

Using the techniques in this book to reignite your self-confidence will transform your life. Such a claim is supported by countless studies confirming that increased self-confidence is directly linked with improved academic performance, better career prospects, and a general increase in happiness and motivation[3]. But you don't need to read academic papers to know that this is true: think of people you know personally who are successful, happy and fulfilled. You'll see that those people exhibit self-confidence. I can say that without meeting them, simply because to be happy and successful, you must also be self-confident.

Think about how you feel now about your own level of self-confidence. Can you identify scenarios and situations that you find particularly confronting? For example, perhaps you find it difficult to:

- Command the attention of large groups and/or strangers.
- Fully express your opinions and ideas in a work or social environment.
- Stand up for your own needs within a relationship.
- Initiate new friendships or relationships.
- Be adventurous, embrace new experiences or journey outside your comfortable places
- Be the leader, be the fun, be the energy rather than hoping someone else will provide all that.

You will have your own unique areas in life where you wrestle with diminished self-confidence. Think carefully about those. You may find this activity difficult. It will make you feel uncomfortable or even embarrassed. That's perfectly understandable: no-one enjoys spending time thinking about their own challenges. Nevertheless, take the time to reflect on these scenarios and then write in your Workbook a brief description of each including how they make you feel: studies confirm that the very act of writing things down helps to clarify your thinking, process your emotions, and allows you to see more clearly what you need to change[4].

You don't need to share this information with anyone else. It's just for you and it's an important first stage in identifying the areas of your life where enhancing your self-confidence will make the greatest difference. These will become your goals as you begin to apply the techniques in this book. Writing them down also allows you to set a baseline against which you can judge subsequent progress. Not too far in the future, you will be amazed when you look back at what you wrote here and you are able to see how far you have succeeded in transforming your life.

Remember: no matter what level of confidence you have now, you were naturally confident once. You had not accumulated self-doubt or fears. You were born with immense potential and with a natural sense of it. But through time, experiences and your interpretations, that sense became suppressed. Now we begin your journey back to self-confidence by undoing the things that eroded it.

2

WHAT HAPPENED?

You can have anything you want if you are willing to give up the belief that you can't have it.

– Dr. Robert Anthony

How's your self-image? Does it need an uplift? Do you want to regain the youthful freedom, energy, and enthusiasm that comes from having confidence? If you do, you're not alone. Lots of people experience a lack of self-confidence that impacts every area of their lives. Improving your confidence is a worthy goal and one that leads to profound life changes. Understanding how to do that is what this book is about. But first, let's see if we can figure out how you arrived where you are now.

In the previous chapter we explained that reduced confidence isn't something innate, it's something that you learned. You started out confident as a child but that confidence was gradually eroded. What caused that to happen?

I will be talking here in general terms about some of the most common roots of a lack of self-confidence. When you are reading, I want you to think about how these things relate to your life. Can you identify with any of these as the roots of your self-image or can you see other causes in your life? You'll find helpful related exercises in your Workbook.

LIFE EXPERIENCES

For the vast majority of people, a lack of self-confidence is something directly linked to negative life experiences. The factors that may lead to a lack of self-confidence are varied and complex, but some of the most common causes are:

> **Trauma.** Abuse in any form, whether it is sexual, physical or emotional can leave us with diminished feelings of self-worth and a lack of confidence. If you find yourself

replaying traumatic experiences of abuse or being constantly troubled by feelings of anxiety, embarrassment or guilt about events in your past, the practical techniques presented in this book will provide enormous benefit. Whilst it's not a replacement for professional mental health advice and treatment, this book will provide a new focus for your attention instead of being mired in unconstructive thoughts from past experiences.

Negative experiences during education. School can be a challenging time. It can even be the root of a lack of confidence in later life. The reasons you may feel unhappy at school can take many forms:

Bullying is sadly common in schools despite many efforts to reduce or eradicate it. Bullying and the humiliation it causes may leave you with life-long mental associations about how you look, your physical or mental abilities or your ability to form friendships and become part of social groups. When I was at school my parents were comparatively poor compared to those of many of my friends. They simply couldn't afford to provide me with the expensive clothes that many of my peers wore. That made me look and feel different, and that in turn led to my exclusion from many social groups. Well after the bullying stops at school, the trauma that it leaves behind can affect how we interact with the world for years to come.

Of course, bullying doesn't just happen in school: harassment at work or in social groups is also a form of bullying, as is a peer group that, for any reason, fails to show you reasonable respect and acceptance. Any action taken by another person that leaves you feeling humiliated, diminished and that undermines your feelings of self-confidence may be a form of bullying. However, you may be surprised to learn that many famous and successful people were the victims of bullying. Many of the movies of Director Steven Spielberg feature outsiders. That's partly because he was the victim of childhood bullying. US Presidents Bill Clinton and Barack Obama have both described being bullied as children. Controversial radio and television personality Howard Stern first used humor as a way of deflecting bullies. Bullying is a problem, but it doesn't have to define your life or hold you back. Has bullying left behind an imprint that still affects how you feel about yourself? Chapter 15 has got some powerful information to transform your perception of what those old events mean.

Bad teaching style. Fiction is full of inspirational teachers who motivate their pupils to succeed. There are such people, but unfortunately there are also teachers who do the precise opposite. Up to the age of fourteen, I did well academically at school, scoring at or near the highest levels in every subject. Then I was assigned to the classes of a particular mathematics teacher. In retrospect I can see that he was extremely intelligent and very, very knowledgeable about mathematics. I can also see that, for whatever reason, he didn't like me at all and he wasn't a great teacher. He was impatient, dismissive, and occasionally downright rude when I failed to understand something. He often compared me unfavorably (and publicly) to more able members of my class. I learned to keep my head down and my mouth shut in his classes. As a result, and for the first time in school, I fell further and further behind until I finally failed the final mathematics examination, the only final exam in which I did not achieve one of the highest grades. That teacher taught me to feel stupid and left me with a life-long aversion to anything that involves advanced mathematics. I know that many, many other people have experienced the same impact from being exposed to bad teaching and this can lead to a lack of self-confidence in specific areas in later life. In Chapter 4 I'll share with you what I've learnt that has dramatically shifted my view of the world since Mr Walker took his own issues out on me.

Unrealistic parental expectations. My parents, particularly my father, made it clear that they expected me to "*do well*" at school. If I failed to meet their expectations, they assumed that it was because I wasn't working hard enough. When my marks in, for example, mathematics started to slip, they simply berated me for not putting in sufficient effort. I wasn't able to articulate just how the style of one particular teacher was making me feel. I believed my parents and assumed that the fault was mine, which simply made me feel even more stupid and inadequate. As a young teenager, I simply didn't have the intellectual or emotional capacity to see that the fault wasn't all mine. Over time this eroded my confidence to the point where I began to dread report cards. Chapter 8 contains the ultimate antidote to this way of thinking.

Discrimination due to gender, religion, race, and sexual orientation. For a very long time, it was assumed that the brains of men and women were somehow different. It's only relatively recent research that proves conclusively that there are no significant functional differences between male and female brains[5]. So why do men and women often behave differently? That seems to be because women learn to have different expectations that may lead to a lack of self-confidence and different behaviors. In particular, studies show that: *"Women have been socialized* (conditioned) *into understanding that what is most important is that they be perceived as likable and agreeable.*[6]*"* Being "*agreeable*" may involve subsuming your own opinions, needs, and ideas to those of others. That leads directly to a decrease in self-confidence. Conversely, being assertive may be perceived as somehow unfeminine. Discrimination due to religious affiliation, racial background or sexual orientation may also lead to a person having distorted perceptions of their own worth, abilities, and expected roles. At the age of fifteen, Constance Baker Motley was turned away from a public beach in America because she was black. That experience created her interest in fighting discrimination and she went on to become the first black US Federal Judge. In Ireland, decades of unrest, violence, and murder were caused by antagonism between Catholic and Protestant communities. This was finally ended in 2005 and since that time these groups have learned to live in peace. Any form of discrimination can erode self-confidence, but all can be overcome. You'll learn how to do this in Chapter 16.

Relationships. Social and work relationships have a direct effect on feelings of confidence. Feelings of confidence also enable more positive social and work relationships. Positive, supportive relationships make you feel more confident[7]. Negative relationships, where the other person doesn't provide support or understanding, criticizes and blames you, all steal your self-confidence. There are all kinds of reasons why someone acts that way within a relationship, and they aren't necessarily because of you. That other person could be forcing their own insecurities and problems onto you. You can't change that other person. You can only change yourself. If you find yourself in a negative relationship of any kind, you need to think about reducing your time with that person. We'll be talking in more detail about how to examine your relationships and how to foster those that are positive in Chapter 9. For the moment, consider that bad relationships are a major source of reduced self-confidence.

The Dunning-Kruger Effect and Imposter Syndrome. Albert Einstein famously said:

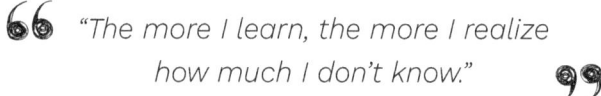

> *"The more I learn, the more I realize how much I don't know."*

He was right, and this fact is now recognized in psychology as a cognitive bias known as the Dunning-Kruger Effect[8]. In short, this effect means that, when you know relatively little about something, you have a tendency to overestimate your own ability and knowledge leading to over-confidence. As you learn more, you begin to understand how little you really know and how much you have to learn and your confidence initially falls.

Imagine that you are learning to drive a stick shift for the first time. When you start out, the simple fact that you can pull away from rest without stalling the engine makes you feel pretty good. As you gain experience, you won't even think about that and instead, you will start to focus on the overall experience of driving. At that point, trying to master the car's controls while remaining aware of everything else happening on the road can

The more I learn, the more I realize how much I don't know.

seem overwhelming. The confidence you had right at the start is replaced by nervousness about how much more you still have to learn.

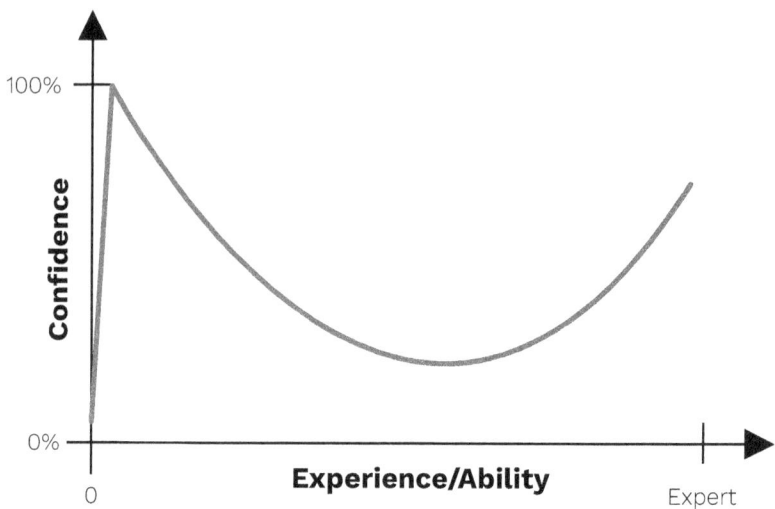

The same thing applies to learning almost anything new. Your confidence is high when you begin because you tend to overestimate your knowledge and ability. As you start to learn how much there is still to do, your confidence drops and bottoms-out. Then, as your experience and knowledge grow further, your confidence gradually recovers and rises again. When you are at the bottom of the curve, where you have just enough knowledge and experience to understand how much more you have to learn and your confidence is at its lowest, you may suffer from something known as *"imposter syndrome."* This happens when your confidence is much lower than it should be given your level of ability and experience. Imposter syndrome is particularly prevalent if you compare yourself to others at this stage.

Who stole my confidence? Accepting that your current level of self-confidence is not maximized is an essential starting point for making positive change. But you also need to understand where that level of confidence comes from. Did the bullying you suffered from at school or the impact of a bad teacher affect your confidence? Do negative social or work relationships undermine your confidence? Does your gender, religion or race make you predisposed to attitudes that undermine your confidence? Are you simply in the process of learning something new and you find yourself currently at the bottom of the confidence vs experience/knowledge curve?

When you read the examples in this chapter of what may have eroded your confidence, some may resonate for you. Using the techniques in this book, you <u>will</u> be able to restore your birth-right confidence.

You didn't just wake up one morning and find that you lacked self-confidence. Likewise, your self-confidence will take thought and action to restore. Confidence (or the lack of it) is created by a cycle of behavior and reinforcement that builds over time. It's important to understand how those cycles operate and how you can ensure that you engage with an upward cycle that will increase your confidence. That's what we'll be looking at in the next Chapter.

If you haven't already, please take time now to do the exercises in your Workbook. They are extremely powerful.

3

THE CONFIDENCE CYCLES. "GOING UP?"

"Procrastinators are self-handicappers: rather than risk failure, they prefer to create conditions that make success impossible, a reflex that of course creates a vicious cycle."

– James Surowiecki

You have heard the saying *"everyone has a book in them."* The implication is that all of us have the capacity to write a book. In truth, the only difference between a writer and a would-be writer is that the writer writes while the would-be writer doesn't. It's a fundamental and critical difference and precisely the same thing applies to the would-be entrepreneur, sportsperson, or anyone else aiming to change their lives in a positive way. Attaining confidence in anything is about actually doing that thing and then following a positive and ascending cycle of action and reinforcement. Increased confidence enables you to take effective action. Taking successful action leads to increasing confidence and so on.

Far too many people are fearful of taking action. They may want to change, but they are locked in a descending cycle of diminishing self-confidence. This leads either to a lack of action through procrastination or to failed or sabotaged actions that in turn lead to increased negativity and diminished confidence. If a person allows themselves to remain in this cycle, they also remain in the *"would-be"* category. They will never build the confidence needed to take the actions required to change their lives.

It is important to understand that whether you are in an ascending or descending cycle of self-confidence isn't a matter of chance or external circumstances. It's about how you think about the situations in your life and how you act in response to them. It's a choice you make, even though you may not recognize that.

You <u>can</u> make the choice to move from a negative, descending cycle to a positive, ascending cycle.

First, you have to recognize what these cycles look like.

THE DESCENDING SELF-CONFIDENCE CYCLE

The descending self-confidence cycle looks like this:

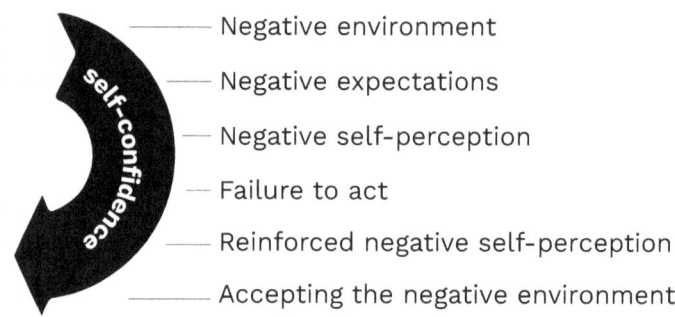

- Negative environment
- Negative expectations
- Negative self-perception
- Failure to act
- Reinforced negative self-perception
- Accepting the negative environment

You are in a negative environment. This could be a home with critical or unsupportive parents, a school where you are bullied or influenced by bad teachers, a destructive relationship, or a work environment that is hostile, negative and unsupportive. Perhaps the most prevalent one of all is spending time with friends whose behavior and mindset are negative. Being in such an environment means that,

You have negative expectations. Being in a negative environment where other people talk about failing themselves and seem to expect you to fail will lead you to have negative expectations about your own abilities such as "*I can't do this*" or "*I'm certain to fail if I try this*". Then,

You develop a negative self-perception. You begin to think negatively not just about specific situations but overall about your own abilities. You may begin to think of yourself as stupid, ineffective, lacking in ability, or incapable of improvement. Negative expectations plus a negative self-perception leads to a dramatic drop in self-confidence. This leads to,

Failure to act or limited or sabotaged action. You are so demoralized and so lacking in self-confidence that you resort to procrastination to avoid what you see as inevitable failure: rather than take an action you believe will fail, you do nothing. If you are forced to take action when you feel this way, you may respond by doing as little as possible (limited action) or you may even try to fail as quickly as possible (sabotaging your own actions). This leads to,

Your negative self-perception is reinforced. Your inability to take action or your failure when you do act simply serve to reinforce your feelings of worthlessness and stupidity. Then,

You come to accept that you belong in a negative environment. Belonging is an extremely powerful psychological concept. Humans are social creatures. We have an innate need for connection with other people. This fosters a yearning to belong, to a social group, a way of thinking, or even a place. However, that sense of belonging brings with it a need to see how we fit. It means assessing our own worth within a particular connection. If we feel ineffective and worthless, we will seek an environment where we see that as appropriate. In other words, we identify ourselves as belonging in a negative environment. And we're back at the start of the cycle ...

INSTANT AUTHENTIC SELF CONFIDENCE

This is really important { Remember, this is a cycle: it doesn't have a beginning or an end and you can join it at any point. When you're in it, every succeeding stage further undermines your confidence. Every new trip round the cycle makes the situation even worse. The opposite of the descending cycle is:

THE ASCENDING SELF-CONFIDENCE CYCLE

The ascending self-confidence cycle looks like this:

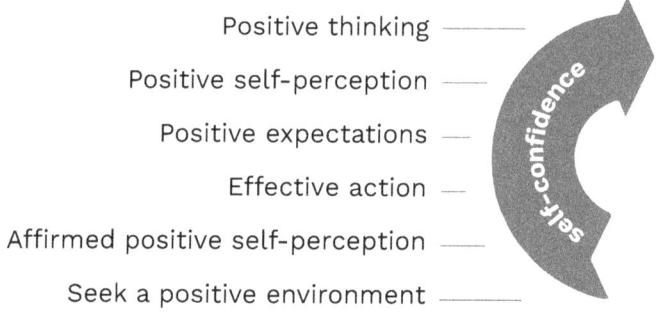

Positive thinking
Positive self-perception
Positive expectations
Effective action
Affirmed positive self-perception
Seek a positive environment

self-confidence

Positive thinking. You make a conscious effort to adopt positive ways of thinking. The techniques in this book, for example, help you to do this. This is not the same as wishful thinking or simply ignoring setbacks or failures. Positive thinking means looking for the best in any given situation and using this to see opportunities to learn and grow. This leads to,

Positive self-perception and positive expectations. Adopting the habit of positive thinking allows you to identify your own strengths. Focusing on these allows you to begin seeing yourself as capable, talented, and effective in what you do. Again, this isn't about creating unrealistic expectations. You really <u>are</u> all those things. Positive thinking just helps you to see that. With that knowledge, you expect to succeed in what you do. This overall positivity leads to,

Effective action. Taking action is at the heart of improving self-confidence. You cannot become self-confident just by thinking or talking about it. You must use your positive mindset to allow you to undertake actions that achieve what you set out to do. Every time you do this, you increase your competence, knowledge and experience. These positive outcomes lead to,

Affirmed positive self-perception. Every time that you act successfully and with deliberate intent, your self-perception and self-confidence are boosted. You will then find that you approach new actions with the feeling that "*I can do this!*" That attitude makes it far more likely that you will succeed. When successful action becomes a habit, you will find that you,

Seek a positive environment. When you are confident in your ability to take effective action, you will seek and rightfully expect an environment that provides support and encouragement. You will feel that you rightfully belong in such a place, with such people. When you find yourself there, this will further enhance your positive thinking …

Just like the descending cycle, this ascending self-confidence cycle can be entered at any point. Each stage increases positivity and self-confidence. Each cycle makes you stronger and more confident.

Do you recognize yourself or your current circumstances in either of these cycles?

 Your Workbook has a single, simple, powerful question to ask you. Go take a look at that now.

Remember: you are not a helpless victim of circumstance or a passive observer of your own life. That's how it can feel when you are in a descending self-confidence cycle. The truth is that you are in control of your life. You can make a conscious decision to change the way that you think and to increase your self-confidence. No matter how unconfident you might feel right now you are one small decision away from getting yourself on to the ascending self-confidence cycle.

Move on to Part 2 to learn how to do this now …

PART 2

Powerful New Ways To Think

Self-confidence isn't just feeling good about yourself. It's the basis of how you interact with the world and a fundamental element of success in any endeavor. It isn't about being arrogant: confident people are aware of their imperfections and they consider the needs of others, but they learn to assert their own needs and opinions and to develop a sense of their own self-worth. One that isn't based on the opinions of other people. They learn to value themselves and to be willing to try new experiences and new adventures.

Self-confidence is an essential life skill and the underpinning for anything you achieve. If you want to succeed, you must be self-confident. In the first part of this book, you learned how a lack of self-confidence can hold you back. You also discovered how your own self-confidence may have been eroded. In this part, I present techniques you can use to restore your self-confidence and practical strategies for integrating these into your everyday life.

Your new, self-confident life begins here.

BUT I'M A FISH!

Discover Where You're Already Great

Never trust your fears, they don't know your strength.

– Athena Singh

<u>If a fish were to judge its own worth based on its ability to climb a tree, it would have a horrible self-image. But that's precisely</u> what a great many people do. Instead of basing their feelings of self-worth on the many things they are good at, instead they focus predominantly on things they are bad at.

Musically, I'm a complete dunce. Though I have tried several times, I can't play any musical instrument, I have no sense of rhythm and when I try to sing or whistle, people leave the room. Probably as a direct result, I'm a terrible dancer too. I'm very jealous of people who can do these things. My beautiful wife is the precise opposite. She can pick up virtually any instrument, even one she hasn't seen before, and almost immediately pick out a tune. She can sing. She can dance.

Once, she talked me into attending tango classes. After all, she assured me, all I'd have to do was follow instructions and listen to the music. And surely, anyone can do that? After just two lessons of forgetting the steps, losing my place and bumping into other students, the instructor took me aside and gently suggested that, you know, not everyone can do this and perhaps I'd like to consider learning some other new skill?

If I based my sense of self-worth on my musical ability, I'd probably never leave the house. Instead, I have come to accept that I'll never be able to dance like John Travolta or play the guitar like Ry Cooder. But that doesn't make me feel worthless because I know there are other things that I can do competently, in fact, brilliantly. For all her musical ability my wife, for example, can't dismantle and rebuild a motorcycle the way that I can ...

This is not frivolous. It's actually very important. Your sense of self-worth, the feeling that you are a person who deserves to be treated with respect, is directly tied to your self-confidence. If your sense of self-worth is low, it's going to be very hard to increase your self-confidence.

You derive your sense of self-worth to a large extent by comparing positive and negative aspects of your abilities. But if you determine your self-worth by focusing on things that you are bad at, it will be low. The answer isn't to try to make yourself better at these things: I know that no matter how hard I try, I'll never be able to turn myself into a great singer. Instead, you need to re-calibrate the way that you think and focus on the things that you are good at.

Traditional education is one of the reasons that we learn to base our self-worth on the wrong things. Most education systems are based on the notion that all children must learn everything. But we know that just isn't possible. A girl who is great at mathematics but struggles with art may be judged a failure. That's not just unfair, it risks undermining her sense of self-worth by making her judge her abilities by her failure in art, not by her success in mathematics.

The reason that tends to happen is due to something called negativity bias (also known as positive-negative asymmetry). Several psychological studies[9] have confirmed that our brains seem to be hard-coded to give more weight to negative stimuli. Psychologists believe this is a throwback to our ancient past where the ability to quickly identify threats and danger was an important survival mechanism.

Due to negativity bias, negative feedback in an art class will probably have a more profound impact on that girl than praise in mathematics classes and she will unconsciously assign more importance to her failure than her success when judging her self-worth. Negative events are also far more likely to gain our attention than positive experiences and we often base our decisions more on negative factors[10]. In recognition of this, new methods of teaching are being introduced that focus on *"strength-based learning,"* finding out what children are good at and focusing on those strengths rather than trying to overcome weaknesses.

You can use a similar approach to support your journey to self-confidence. You must accept that there are things that you are not particularly good at, but everyone also has things they are good at. However, negativity bias tends to make us overlook these. We are all very familiar with our weaknesses, but often less able to identify our strengths. Take a moment now to think about this. There's an exercise in your Workbook that will provoke some new and helpful thoughts.

Once you have completed that exercise, you can use this knowledge to boost your sense of self-worth. For example:

> **Celebrate your strengths.** You're good at some things. Knowing what those are is great, because you can learn to use them more. But take a minute to celebrate them too. It's awesome that you have a unique set of skills and abilities. Feel good about that! OK, I know that I'll never be able to dance. But if your car won't start, I'm your guy! That knowledge makes me feel good.

Listen to yourself, not other people. Other people often don't understand what your strengths are. Only you do. Other people probably don't understand your true goals or values either. If you pay too much attention to other people, you'll lose focus on what matters to you. Assess yourself on how much you're growing, learning and changing, not on what others seem to think of you. Your opinion of yourself matters. Other people's opinion of you doesn't.

Find positives, even in the negatives. Even the most successful people suffer failures and setbacks. You will too. But you have an option in how you respond to that. For example, James Dyson is an incredibly successful entrepreneur. But he went through years of failure before he created his best-selling vacuum cleaner. In an interview, he said something really interesting about that:

 You never learn from success, but you do learn from failure[11].

That's really important and absolutely right. When you succeed, you tend not to think about it. But every failure is a valuable learning opportunity. Perhaps you can't really succeed until you have learned from failing along the way? Learn to see failure as an opportunity for even greater success. Learn to find positives even in negatives.

Savor those positive moments. When you find opportunities to use your strengths effectively, take the time to recognize that and to appreciate it. Fully engage in those moments to create positive memories that increase your sense of self-worth.

You never learn from success, but you do learn from failure.

INSTANT AUTHENTIC SELF CONFIDENCE

There is one other thing that you need to avoid in order to increase your sense of self-worth: don't be tempted to compare yourself to other people. That's counter-productive for a number of reasons but it may also be unrealistic. The image that other people project may be false and you may be comparing yourself to something that's unattainable or simply an illusion.

5

IT'S ALL FAKE

When The Standard Is 'Fake' Don't Use That As Your Guide

Comparison is the death of joy.

– Mark Twain

A great deal of what you see on social media is fake. You already know that, right? When someone is talking to you about their life, they're usually only giving you the edited highlights, the good bits. You know that too, don't you? So, how come you spend so much time comparing yourself to fake versions of other people's lives?

OK, I know, we all do it. I'm as prone as anyone else. If I see a guy on social media looking really sharp: good clothes, nice tan, wry smile, I can't help but feel a twinge of envy. Especially if I'm staring at my computer in my old t-shirt and sweatpants. I think that's probably normal. But I have come to understand two things that are really important here.

First, what I see on social media or hear in casual conversation is just a snapshot. It's a single moment in another person's life. Probably chosen to make them look good. Not everyone looks good all the time. Everyone spends time in old t-shirts and sweatpants. Maybe what I'm seeing or hearing is even completely fake: photoshopped, manipulated, and edited for maximum effect. Second, and most importantly, I can choose how to react to this information. I can choose to be disheartened because I feel like I'll never be as handsome/rich/cool/well-dressed as that other person. Or I can be inspired to buy new clothes, get a haircut and generally improve the way that I present.

You can do the same, to reject the fake and to make a choice about whether to be inspired or depressed by the rest.

The 2021 HBO documentary *Fake Famous* by Nick Bilton looked at a social experiment which took three unknown young people in Los Angeles and attempted to turn them into social media influencers with vast followings. This involved using professional photographers and videographers to create media suggesting that these three people lived fascinating and full lives. It also used technology to buy fake followers: nothing generates on-line interest more quickly than a large social media following.

It worked. All three of the participants were able to generate large followings. One, actress Dominique Druckman, discovered that her new-found Internet celebrity actually helped her to find acting roles. However, all three were troubled by the fake nature of the personas portrayed on social media. Even the creator and director of the show, Nick Bilton, expressed concerns about what was happening:

> *"And what I realized was the whole point of influencing is to make you feel bad. It is to make you say, you don't get to live the life I live. You don't get to go on these fancy vacations. You don't get to get these free products, you have to go work for them.*[12]*"*

Everyone knows that social media is fake and studies confirm it. One[13] suggested that anything up to 45% of all Instagram accounts may be fake, up to 55% of all Instagram influencers used some form of fraud in their posts, and over 66% of *"mega-influencers"* (those with more than one million followers) regularly employ fraudulent practices. However, social media fakery isn't just about these influencers. It's something we all do.

Think about your own social media posts. Do they present a balanced, warts-and-all narrative of your life? Or do they show a curated version that highlights the positive stuff? That's what most of us do. You may have been in the middle of having a terrible argument with your partner, but the picture you post showing you both smiling together at a romantic location probably won't mention that. Your posts may show that great meal you shared in a restaurant last week but probably not the beans on toast you ate alone last night because you just couldn't muster the energy to prepare anything more complex.

Unwittingly and often unconsciously, we present the best possible view of ourselves and our lives for public presentation. That is normal and it isn't confined to social media. To most people, we try to project a positive image. We find it easier to share positive rather than negative emotions. It is often only to our closest and most intimate friends and family that we will admit that we are struggling with elements of our lives. The fact that almost all of us continually present a carefully manufactured persona can be an issue because we all have a tendency to compare ourselves to other people. If what we are comparing to is fake or at least curated, it can make us feel that everyone else is smarter, more successful, more attractive, and more capable than we are.

Social Comparison theory was first proposed in the 1950s by American psychologist Leon Festinger. This theory suggests that we all have an innate drive to judge ourselves by comparison to other people. Festinger described the theory based on how we tend to evaluate ourselves compared to our peers, but social media has vastly expanded the range of people to whom we may be tempted to make comparisons. Now, we're tempted to compare ourselves to the whole bloody world! No wonder we get discouraged! It becomes a particular problem if we compare ourselves to a fake persona presented by another person. That can leave us feeling insecure and inadequate. As Pastor Steve Furtick rightly notes:

> *"The reason we struggle with insecurity is because we compare our behind-the-scenes with everyone else's highlight reel.*[14]*"*

One thing to remember is that often, the people who make the most effort to project themselves as successful, wealthy, attractive, etc., are actually the people who are most in need of validation and support. These people often do not create a false persona in order to deceive: they do this because unconsciously they see it as the only way in which they can become deserving of respect, affection, and love.

Being inspired by another person is fine. Inspiration is about learning from another person and it tells you that you too can accomplish what they have done. It can provide motivation for change and it's about looking at your own life. Comparing yourself to another person is not productive. Comparison puts the emphasis on the wrong person. You can only control your own life, and that's where you need to focus your energy.

To avoid becoming mired in unhelpful comparison:

> **Be aware.** One of the best ways to combat the potential ill-effects of comparison is to be aware when you're doing it. Instead, make a deliberate effort to switch your thinking to yourself. Think about your goals, your achievements, and your strengths. They're awesome! They matter more than what any other person is doing. Your progress towards your goals is what defines you. What other people appear to be doing is irrelevant.

Take a break from social media. Try spending a week without visiting any social media site. How would that make you feel? Would it allow your feelings of self-worth to increase? Would it reduce the likelihood of you feeling inadequate or lacking achievement? Make phone-free times during the day and phone-free zones in your home. Turn off notifications or even just turn off your phone altogether. Measure how those things make you feel.

Don't chase the unattainable. Many people project a completely false image of themselves and their lives. If you find yourself comparing yourself unfavorably to someone else, take a step back and try to think about their real lives. Are you comparing yourself to something that's real? We know that much of what other people project is fake, or at least heavily edited. You may feel envious of that new car your friend has bought, but think about the debt they are building. You may be a little jealous of that photo of a couple you know on a romantic break, but is that a true reflection of their relationship? What's the point of making a comparison to something that's fictional?

Compare yourself to yourself. Using the guidance in this book, you are going to change for the better. You are going to become more self-confident and this will allow you to achieve things that would have seemed impossible when you started out. Recognize that by comparing your old self without self-confidence to your new approach. See how you are able to accomplish things now that might have terrified you before. That's the only comparison that will help to increase your self-confidence.

Remember that there is always enough success to go round. One of the reasons that comparison to other people can make us unhappy is that we seem to have an innate drive to compete coupled with an unconscious feeling that another person's success has a negative impact on us. That's a fallacy. No matter how much someone else succeeds, there is still success left over for us. If someone else achieves success, feel good for them, but stay focused on moving towards achieving your own success.

Although comparison to others is pointless and unhelpful, that certainly doesn't imply that you shouldn't pay attention to other people. You can be inspired by what others achieve. You just need to pick the right people. And here's a thought: that probably doesn't include people bragging about their own success on social media or in real life. Look at what people actually do, not what they say, before you pick them as a source of inspiration.

To find people worth paying attention to, the LearnWell Community is full of them.

Looking at other people is actually fascinating. Once you learn to step past the facade and see what's really going on, you can learn a great deal. That's what we're looking at in the next chapter.

6

LOOK AT THEM

Find Out Who Is The Most Important Person To Pay Attention To. (It's Not You)

The way you overcome shyness is to become so wrapped up in something that you forget to be afraid.

– Claudia Lady Bird Johnson

One of the most common issues related to a lack of self-confidence is a concern that other people will see how lacking in confidence we are. We become anxious about appearing to be anxious! In extreme cases, this may lead to Social Anxiety Disorder (SAD) where every social interaction becomes a terrifying ordeal. Even for people who aren't affected to that extent, a lack of self-confidence can cause shyness and that can have a pronounced effect on how we interact with other people.

Anxious people tend to overestimate the degree to which other people notice the physical signs of anxiety[15]. In any social situation, people with low self-confidence wrongly assume that more people are looking at them, thinking about them, and talking about them than is actually the case[16]. As a result, they become so focused on concealing signs of their own anxiety that their anxiety is actually increased and their attention is entirely removed from other people, leading to interactions that may seem to be flat or unresponsive.

Fortunately, there is a simple technique that is very effective in dealing with this in any group situation: stop focusing on yourself and start observing other people. People watching is great! You will be amazed at what you see and how differently this makes you feel.

To do this you should make a conscious effort to go beyond the surface to try to see what's going on. We all tend to focus on ourselves in social interactions. What do people think of me? Do I look stupid in this hat? Do I have spinach stuck between my teeth? This focus can make us fail to pay attention to what the other person is saying and how they are presenting.

What I want you to do is to try to forget about yourself and focus on other people. If you're lacking in confidence, you tend to self-obsess, especially when you're with other people. Instead, I want you to really listen to and observe other people. I think you'll see that everyone else is just as uncertain as you are.

Here are some of the most obvious things you'll notice:

Physical "tells." You can perceive a great deal about how someone is just by looking at their body language. Do they look relaxed and confident? Do they look tense, holding themselves very rigidly, clenching their fist(s), clenching their jaw, tapping their feet, and seeming unable to remain still. You can also look for other physical signs of tension such as compulsive smoothing of hair or clothes, nail biting, and skin picking (dermatillomania).

Attention (or the lack of it). There is nothing worse than talking to someone who clearly isn't listening to what you are saying. Conversely, someone who is really paying attention makes you feel good. It may be that someone who isn't listening just isn't interested in you or what you have to say. But it's likely that they are just focussed on themselves, too busy wondering what others may be thinking to really listen. People may also seem disinterested because they feel that sharing emotions, particularly with someone they don't know well, makes them vulnerable.

Need for reassurance. Even in casual conversation, some people have a compulsive need to know that you agree with their point of view. If you disagree, they may find this discomforting and, rather than seeing it as the basis for an expanded conversation and discussion, they may react by withdrawing entirely.

Once you get the hang of it, people-watching is fun. Fun is good, but there is also a serious purpose to this exercise. A lack of confidence is very, very common. If you take the time to really focus on the people you are interacting with, I think you'll see that many of them lack confidence. That's helpful because, if you (mistakenly) believe that everyone is more confident than you, that can leave you feeling excluded and different. If you can see that many people feel as you do, it will become much easier to form meaningful connections.

Doing this may also help you to change how you behave in social situations. If you recognise how irritating it is to talk to someone who doesn't seem to be listening, there is a good chance that you won't do that. It also helps to make sure that you are fully engaged. Instead of worrying about what others may be thinking, you'll find yourself better able to appreciate what's happening right now. Being fully in the present moment as opposed to thinking about the past or future is a great way to connect with others and to boost your self-confidence.

Finally, using a social gathering as a way to observe and make connections with other people will reduce your own anxiety. As the quote at the beginning of this chapter notes, your shyness and anxiety will evaporate as you begin to see social gatherings not as an ordeal but as an opportunity for learning.

INSTANT AUTHENTIC SELF CONFIDENCE

People who lack self-confidence don't just feel uncomfortable in social gatherings. Many other situations may also give rise to feelings of discomfort. But increasing your self-confidence isn't just about learning how to decrease this feeling: it's about coming to embrace discomfort as part of your journey towards a new you. We'll be talking about how discomfort can be your friend in the next chapter.

But before moving on, visit your Workbook for an interesting exercise in people-watching!

7

I'M UNCOMFORTABLE AND I LOVE IT!

How To Slowly Become Bullet-Proof

All great roads are paved with uncomfortable memories.

– Amy Neftzger

When was the last time you felt uncomfortable? I'm not talking here about feeling afraid or apprehensive, but being in a situation where you may have felt awkward or uneasy. The chances are that you felt that way because you were doing something new or something that involved an element of uncertainty. Discomfort is a normal response to certain situations, but some people dread this feeling so much that they try to avoid anything that makes them feel that way.

Feeling discomfort is an inescapable part of growth, learning, and improvement. You can only achieve these things by pushing your own boundaries. That <u>will</u> make you feel uncomfortable. What I want you to understand is that feeling discomfort isn't negative at all. Instead, it's an indication that you are moving forward and making positive progress. Don't regard discomfort as something to be avoided. It's confirmation that you are making progress and thus something to be welcomed and embraced. It's also something that everyone feels: remember in the last chapter how you learned to look for signs of discomfort in other people in social gatherings? No matter how well they are able to conceal it, everyone feels uncomfortable when they are faced with novelty and uncertainty.

Take a physical analogy. You want to increase your fitness and stamina, so you start jogging. After a few days or weeks, you reach a point where you can run for a mile without feeling too tired. What do you do then? You could continue to just run a mile, knowing that you can achieve this without too much physical discomfort. Or you can run two miles. That will make you feel a burn in your legs, you'll be gasping for air, you'll be horribly uncomfortable but ... victorious! Not to mention, it will increase your fitness and stamina. Unless you are willing to stretch, accepting the discomfort that brings, you will not continue to grow.

The same thing applies to any other activity you may undertake, whether it's physical, mental or emotional. As you step outside what comes easily and what you have done before, you will initially feel uncomfortable. If you choose instead to always stay within your comfort zone, you will never feel uncomfortable, but neither will you grow or improve. Every moment of magic ever recorded in history happened outside someone's comfort zone. If you want something great, get used to that space.

Staying within a routine can seem comforting through its familiarity. You probably don't feel at all nervous or apprehensive about your journey to work, simply because you do it every day. It's a routine that you barely have to think about. If you are anything like me, there are probably days when you will arrive at work and, if you think about it at all, you will remember nothing about the journey that brought you there.

However, I started to ask myself whether that was a good thing? Whole elements of my life (and not just the journey to work) simply didn't register at all because they had become wholly routine and completely unchallenging and unmemorable. I began to wonder how I would feel as I approached the end of my life. Would I find that I couldn't recall chunks of it because, like my journey to work, they were so mundane? Was that what I wanted to look back on: a life so without discomfort that it all became a vague mass of half-remembered routine? Is that what you want?

Embracing new experiences doesn't mean that you need to seek out dangerous or risky activities. It's about pushing your boundaries.

Only you know where those lie and only you understand what you need to do to get out of your comfort zone. For some people, that might mean sky-diving or bungee-jumping. For others, it might mean speaking up in front of a group of strangers or attending a social function without a partner. Where your personal boundaries currently lie is not important as long as you are able to recognize them and are willing to push them back.

Trying new, stimulating and challenging things isn't just good for improving your confidence, it also changes the way in which you think and actually changes the way in which your brain is wired. The most intense memories are created by exposure to the new and unfamiliar[17]. This also leads to the release of dopamine, a feel-good chemical, and this helps in the creation of new neural pathways, an essential step towards creating new and more positive behaviors.

Discomfort is an inevitable reaction to unfamiliar situations. If you are going to become more self-confident, you will have to expose yourself to such situations. You will feel uncomfortable. Get used to it. Even better, embrace it as a sign that you are moving beyond the routine. The situations where you feel discomfort are the ones that you will remember when you look back. They are also the situations that will help you to grow and to change. Remember, uncertainty is simply another way of saying *"opportunity."*

The actions you take define you as a person. If those are routine, unmemorable and unchallenging, you cannot grow or learn and you certainly will not become self-confident. And as we will see in the next chapter, taking action is at the heart of positive life change.

YOU'RE GOING TO DIE ... BUT NOT BECAUSE OF THIS

How To Dramatically Increase Your Likelihood Of Success

The critical ingredient is getting off your butt and doing something. It's as simple as that.

— Nolan Bushnell, founder of Atari Inc.

What is the fundamental difference between a successful person and an unsuccessful person? In almost every case, the difference is that the successful person has taken action and the unsuccessful person has not. How you think, about yourself and the world in general, is important: positive thinking is an important step towards self-confidence. But how you act defines how you interact with the world.

In the modern, connected world, we are surrounded by information. That in itself can be a problem because we can confuse learning about something with actually doing it. You can read a book about, for example, how to play tennis. Hell, you can read ten or twenty, but none will move you forward as much as spending an hour with a tennis racket in your hand. If you want to move forward, to learn and to grow, you must take action.

A team of researchers at the Virginia Darden School of Business spent over fifteen years looking at the factors that define the mindset of the most successful entrepreneurs[18]. They noted that the most consistently successful people are those who are willing to take action. That's one of the most significant things that differentiates them from the rest. Lots of people have ideas. Turning those ideas into a successful business means acting. Without action, ideas remain just ideas in business and in every other area of life.

Taking action is challenging. While you are reading books about playing tennis (or starting your own business, or becoming self-confident, or anything else) you can tell yourself that you are making progress. But when you act, you must face up to the possibility that you aren't as good as you thought you were or even that you are entirely mistaken. That's OK. Failing or being wrong do not have to be negatives. Whether you succeed or fail in an endeavor is not as important as the act of trying. One of my favorite quotes on this subject comes from Nelson Mandela:

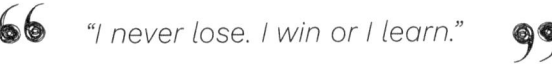
"I never lose. I win or I learn."

If you are going to become self-confident, just reading this book is not enough. You must be willing to act, to take the advice and the techniques here and to actually enact them in your life. Along the way, you are going to fail, because you aren't perfect and you will over-reach or simply not achieve what you set out to do. There are three very important things to remember:

- If you allow the fear of failure to prevent you from taking action, you will never learn, grow, or become self-confident.
- If after failing you give up, you will lose the opportunity to learn. The learning that comes from failure is some of the most valuable information you will ever acquire.
- Every time you fail and carry on, the fear of failure diminishes.

So true!

The pain of regret you will feel if you don't act is far greater than the temporary embarrassment you may feel if you try and fail. Think about regrets you have about your own life. I'm confident you'll see that those that really make you wince are the things that you didn't do, the opportunities you missed. You will almost certainly feel much less pain in recollecting the things you did, even if they weren't 100% successful. If you want to look back without regret, you must be willing to seize new opportunities. That means facing up to the possibility of failure. However, there are things you can do to maximize the chances of any action you take leading to success:

Start with what you already have. You have already identified your own strengths. You already have knowledge and experience. When you are planning any action, think about how you can use those. That means you can begin immediately rather than having to allow time to acquire new skills and knowledge.

Be flexible. When you take action, you are stepping outside your comfort zone and exploring the unknown. As we discussed in the previous chapter, that will make you feel uncomfortable and who knows where it may take you? If you are too rigid in your thinking and expectations, you increase your risk of failure. Suppose that you intend to learn to play golf to increase your fitness. However, you quickly learn that you hate golf and you're not good at it. The walking part was enjoyable. The trees, birds and nature were pleasant but the game itself was just stressful. So, instead of playing golf, you decide that walking is how you'll increase your fitness. That isn't failure: you are still making progress towards your goal but you have switched the way in which you do this. Don't be too rigid in your expectations and be prepared to change direction if needed.

Trust your intuition. We all have hunches, intuitive ideas that don't necessarily seem to originate logically. Whether you call these "*gut instincts*," "*sixth sense*" or whatever, these notions often pop into our minds without conscious effort and seemingly at random. Recently, psychologists have investigated these feelings and discovered that they are far from random: intuitive responses are often formed when our brains subconsciously process information to derive a solution. Even military organizations are beginning to understand that intuition is a powerful tool: the U.S. Office of Naval Research published a paper on this which noted that "*humans can detect and act on unique patterns without consciously and intentionally analyzing them.*[19]" Other studies[20] confirm that decisions made using "*nonconscious emotional information*" arrive faster and are often more accurate and more reliable than those derived from conscious analytical thinking. If you have a gut instinct that a particular course of action may be good for you, act!

Manage risk. Any action carries a risk of failure, that it will not deliver what you had hoped. To minimize the impact of potential failure, think at the very beginning not just of what you stand to gain if the action is successful but also what you stand to lose if it fails. If the action requires an investment of time, how will you feel if it fails? Will you have wasted that time or will you have learned something that will avoid the same failure in future? If the action requires a financial investment, can you afford to lose that money? Anticipating the worst that can happen not only reduces fear, it helps to manage risk by anticipating potential problems and taking action to avoid them.

If you never want to risk failure, there is a simple solution: never do anything new or different. However, if you want to grow, to learn and to become self-confident, you <u>must</u> take action and that <u>will</u> carry a risk of failure. This isn't just a book about ideas. It's a call to action, a set of techniques you can enact to change your life. Along the way, you may experience failure. Get used to it, get over it, and carry on. The only failure that really matters, the only one that causes long-term, insurmountable negative effects, is a failure to take action.

One of the reasons that we often try to avoid even the possibility of failure is that we are (sometimes unconsciously) worried that failure may make other people like and respect us less. That can be a major barrier because we all have a compulsive need to be liked. Unless you learn how to deal with that, it's going to hold you back. That's what we'll explain in the next chapter.

Take a break and spend a few minutes in the Workbook now.

9

THEY DON'T LIKE YOU

How To Find 'Your People'

If you just set out to be liked, you would be prepared to compromise on anything at any time, and you would achieve nothing.

– Margaret Thatcher

Some people just don't like you. Have you noticed? They're not interested in what you're saying. Sometimes they don't seem to be listening at all. They clearly find you uninteresting. They'd obviously prefer to be doing something else and talking to someone else. That's kind of depressing, isn't it? Perhaps it would be best if you just gave up on this whole self-confidence/self-improvement thing and became a hermit instead?

Well, you *could* do that. It's certainly a way of avoiding what other people think of you. But it's probably not practical for most of us. So instead, I want to talk about what's really going on here.

The need to be liked, to receive approval and acceptance, is hard-coded into the human brain. I'm afraid you're stuck with it. That's why you feel bad when someone doesn't like you. So does everyone else. When you hear someone say "*I don't care what people think of me*," you're listening to someone who isn't telling the truth. To you and probably to themselves too. When you read a self-help book or article that tells you to stop caring what other people think, that's impossible too. Instead, you have to learn to listen to the right people and to tune out the rest.

Humans have been social creatures from the very beginning. We learned that in order to survive, we had to live in social groups. Those provided mutual support and protection. Rejection by a group meant that an individual might die. So, we sought reassurance that we were a valued member of a group.

The world has changed since ancient times, but our fundamental need for affirmation and acceptance has not. It begins in earliest childhood when we seek the approval of our parents. It continues through school where we look for positive responses from teachers and friends. In adult life, we seek affirmation from our boss, our partner, our colleagues, and from our friends, relatives, and peers. We even seek approval from strangers through social media. You have a basic need to be liked. But here's an essential truth that you must remember:

Not everyone is going to like you.

That isn't a comfortable thought, but that's just how it is. You don't like everyone, do you? Other people are the same. Their dislike of you may not be rational or fair, but it exists. And right there you have the source of the problem: you have a deep-seated need to be liked, but not everyone likes you. Some people react by trying to change, to become what they think other people want in an effort to be universally liked. They end up obsessed by continually worrying about other people's opinions. It doesn't work because, no matter what you do:

Not everyone is going to like you

I want you to get comfortable with the idea that no matter how you behave or how saintly you are, you <u>cannot</u> have universal approval. If you only retain one idea from this chapter, make it that one. Because to become self-confident, you must overcome the demands of your ancient brain and your need for approval from everyone. You must learn to accept that some people are just never going to like you and to focus your efforts on those who are positive and supportive.

 Stop here briefly for a highly relevant relationship inventory checkup. It's an eye-opening activity in your Workbook.

This begins with learning to value and respect yourself through knowing your own strengths and your weaknesses, as we discussed in Chapter 4. Then, you have to learn to like yourself. Yes, you have faults. We all do. But you have a great many positive traits too. Don't compare yourself to other people and especially don't compare yourself to what you believe other people think of you, because you can never really know.

Suppose you go to a party. You're wearing something different from your usual style: a new outfit, a cool hat or maybe you just have a new haircut. You feel pretty good about yourself. Then you meet someone who makes fun of your new look or is just plain rude. Maybe that's because you do look silly and they want to help you avoid making a fool of yourself. But maybe it's because you actually look pretty darn good and that other person is jealous about the attention you're getting.

That's the problem with seeking approval from others. Some people don't want you to change or improve. That may present a threat to their perceptions of themselves. They take your success as highlighting their own failures and they want everyone to be kept down to their level, though they will never admit that. You can only gain the approval of these people by doing and achieving nothing and making yourself as insignificant as possible. Is that what you want?

Other people respect and like you for what you really are and truly want the best for you. They want to see you change, grow, and learn and they will support your efforts to do those things. These people should be treasured. They are the ones you need to listen to and spend time with. Doing that takes conscious effort.

We all live within a complex and connected web of relationships with family members, friends, colleagues, partners and acquaintances. Not all those relationships are equal and not all are positive. Part of the problem is that these relationships build over time. Sometimes we fail to see imperceptible changes and we can find ourselves in unproductive and negative relationships without being aware of it. There is a simple way to assess the impact a relationship is having on you: think about how spending time with a particular person makes you feel.

That's more difficult than it sounds. Our view of any relationship is colored by the past and by perceptions of a person that may have built over months or even years. It's tricky to separate those past feelings from how that person affects us right now. You have to take a deliberate step back, to make a conscious effort to reflect on how spending time with someone makes you feel.

Some people are generally interested in your plans, aspirations and feelings and they will listen to what you have to say. They are never judgmental and they will probably have plans of their own and they'll share these with you. When you spend time in the company of someone like that, you'll probably laugh together and you will be left feeling energized and optimistic.

Other people are relentlessly negative, though they will cite logic to support their negativity as being "*realistic*". They may be judgmental and they probably won't be truly interested in you or what you have to say. They may even make negative or hurtful comments about you. They may do this in a passive-aggressive way, so that they can deny that they are being negative if you challenge them. When you spend time with someone like that, you'll feel negative, listless, and unenthusiastic.

Relationships are complex and few are as wholly positive or negative as those described above. Most are somewhere in between. The only meaningful measure of a relationship is objectively asking yourself how you feel after spending time with a particular person. Do you feel positive, energetic and enthused? Do you feel drained of energy and negative? How has that person impacted your self-confidence? Does spending time with them make you feel more or less confident?

If you want to boost your self-confidence and increase your positivity, you need to spend more time with people who enable that and less time with those who do the opposite. It really is as simple as that. I'm not suggesting that you suddenly and completely cut certain people out of your life. That's often not possible anyway, particularly in regard to family members and colleagues. But do make a deliberate effort to spend more time with positive, supportive people. And do learn to see negative people and their comments as a reflection of their problems, not your faults.

It's also helpful to take a look at yourself as a friend or colleague. You know what you would look for in a supportive relationship. Do you provide those things? Do you really listen to what people have to say and are you supportive and encouraging about their aspirations? Are you judgmental? Try to make yourself into the kind of friend or colleague that you would value and appreciate. If you can do that, you'll find that positivity attracts positive people.

The better you are as a friend or colleague, the stronger your chances of attracting new friends of the same type.

You need to be liked but, no matter how wonderful you become, you will not be liked by everyone. That's a fundamental fact of life. Accept it, face it and move on. Spend time with people who really like you and care about you. You will still feel the pain of a hurtful comment no matter how self-confident you become. But you will learn to put that in context and to see it not as a reflection of you but of the insecurities and issues of the person making it. And fortunately, there is a particular antidote to that pain that can also improve all your relationships and boost your positivity and self-confidence. It's something that you used to be pretty good at, but that you have probably forgotten how to do. It's called having fun…

10

GIGGLE. A LOT MORE

The Best Way To Never Be Boring!

> *When you have confidence, you can have a lot of fun. And when you have fun, you can do amazing things.*
>
> *– Joe Namath*

This captures the whole point and purpose of this book

You've stopped having fun, haven't you? People think of you as a serious person. In some ways, that's good. But being unrelentingly serious can also make you hard to be around. When was the last time you really enjoyed yourself? When you did something for the sheer joy of it. When you laughed out loud and made others around you do the same. When you felt completely relaxed and totally immersed in an activity for no other reason than it made you feel good. Can you remember?

If you're anything like most adults, you'll probably struggle to recall. Because most of us have come to believe that fun is for kids. Perhaps it feels like a waste of time and something faintly selfish. Or even illicit, like sneaking off from school to go to the movies. We come to believe that fun is the direct opposite of the energy, drive and passion needed for success. Even the definition of fun calls it something frivolous:

"Not for a serious purpose[20]."

Sheesh! OK, I know, the responsibilities of adulthood can seem short of fun. Whether it's managing money and bills, advancing your career, or just watching the news, it can seem like there isn't a lot of space for fun. And even if you could find the time, well, surely there is something more productive you could be doing than just having fun?

Stop!

Fun is good for you. It leads to increased production of endorphins, dopamine, and oxygen, all of which make you feel good and make your brain more receptive to focus and learning. Having fun reduces stress[21] and that in turn reduces anxiety and helps you to sleep better. Being fun also makes you more attractive to other people[22] and it even reduces your perception of pain[23]. Having fun is fundamental to living a fulfilling life.

You used to have fun. As a kid, you played and you did things just for amusement and enjoyment. You probably laughed a lot more too. Now, the needle on your fun-gauge rarely twitches above zero. That's a major problem and it's something we're going to have to change.

Take a deep breath and a step back. The world is a big place. You are only one tiny element of it. Your view of your own significance is wildly inflated. That's absurd. Actually, it's rather funny. An incredibly powerful way of boosting your self-confidence is to become aware of your own insignificance and to learn to smile about that. That helps to avoid a false and pompous view of your own worth. It also helps you to see that having fun doesn't make you a less valued, respected, and loved person.

A long time ago, I worked in a large organization. We had regular, lengthy, serious progress meetings where we took turns to present reports. We discussed important stuff, but man, those meetings left me feeling dazed and exhausted! One evening, I watched a musical movie, one of the old ones where characters suddenly burst into song. I happened to mention it in passing to a colleague the following day. I said how wonderful it would be if in real life we could express ourselves through song.

I didn't really think any more about it, but that colleague attended the next meeting. To my utter surprise and delight, he delivered his entire progress report in song. People smiled. People laughed. Energy levels in the room soared. Of all the many, many progress meetings I attended during six years in that role, that's the one I remember best. It was fun! And we got more done than in any other meeting I attended. My colleague wasn't afraid of looking silly. But other people's respect and liking for him only increased after our memorably musical meeting. How would you feel if someone did this in a meeting?

You don't have to burst into song to create fun (though if you can sing, hey, why not give it a try at your next meeting?). But do feel free to be outrageous: wear fancy dress to your next office party or deliver your next monthly report as a poem. Do something to shake up the routine in a fun way. Make people smile!

You will have to set aside what is probably a false view of your own importance and dignity, but you may be astonished at the response. Doing things that provide fun for you and other people matter! They don't only make you feel better within yourself, they make you a more engaging and interesting companion, colleague and friend. Spend less time worrying what other people think and learn to take yourself a little less seriously!

 Turn to your Workbook now. There's something truly exciting waiting for you there!

You are also really good at the things you enjoy. Best-selling author Stephen King was asked what drove him to write. His answer is worth remembering:

 "I did it for the buzz. I did it for the pure joy of the thing. And if you can do it for the joy, you can do it forever.[24]*"*

He's right. If you do something you enjoy, if you are having fun, you can sustain the effort for longer and keep your focus more intensely. Back in Chapter 4, we talked about identifying your own strengths. Very often, the things that we're good at are also the things we enjoy: having fun at something encourages us to spend more time developing our skills and abilities. That makes us feel good which makes us want to do it more. It's a self-reinforcing cycle. If you focus on strengths that also involve things that you enjoy, you will increase your chances of success exponentially. Don't give in to the feeling that, if you're having fun, you aren't also doing something valid and important.

<u>But never feel that doing something just for fun isn't also worthwhile.</u>

Look, don't tell anyone, but I enjoy building plastic model kits. I was passionate about this as a kid, so it involves a large chunk of nostalgia. I can completely lose myself for hours at a time as I try to turn a small pile of plastic parts into a representation of a tank or an aircraft. It's completely pointless, except as a source of enjoyment. Objectively, I know that's good for me. I find it fun and relaxing and I know that it helps me sleep and that makes me better able to find the energy to do the other productive stuff during the day.

But I'm slightly embarrassed about admitting that I spend my evenings building old model kits. It isn't a cool hobby, I don't make money from it, it doesn't improve my fitness and I can't really justify it in any rational way. I do it simply because I enjoy it. What I have come to realize is that is a perfectly good reason. Enjoyment is good for me. If people want to laugh at me, I laugh right along with them. If people want to think that I'm a nerd, well, I probably am. But I keep right on building those old model kits. Just for fun ...

What do you do just for fun? ???

Having fun is an essential part of living a full and satisfying life. Being fun is part of what makes you human and it is probably an element of what other people find loveable about you. Never be afraid of doing what you enjoy or looking silly. Those things won't make people respect or love you less: only pomposity and an inflated sense of your own importance can do that.

Most of all: have fun!

11

WHO ARE YOU?

The Chance To Create The Best Version Of Yourself

What is the one message that only you can give? It's your story.

– J.R. Rim

It's time to drop the act.

Who are you? Really? There is someone we see but there is someone else beneath that surface, dying to emerge.

So, who are you? Not your name. Not your job title. Not how others would describe you. You.

Life can contort us such that we become an altered version of ourselves. We adopt characteristics that we glean from the strongest influences in our lives and we forsake our true character as though our altered version is superior. As we move further from the center of who we are, what we're good at, what we love doing and who we love to be around, we start to become estranged from ourselves. At this point, the likelihood that we'll maintain a strong identity is slim.

We become unnecessarily obsessed with comparing ourselves to who we want to be. Instead of allowing our true, vivid, authentic selves to emerge.

Powerful characters are authentic versions of themselves. They have an identity that is consistent and clear. Even, frankly, if it's weird or different than most. It's powerful. It's unshakable and it's not prone to influence by others.

I like nothing more than spending time with my family. I'm the silliest, boldest, truest version of myself when I'm with them. I'm not pretending to be anyone else. I'm fully immersed in my true character and it feels so good. I'm free when I'm with them and I'm boldly confident as a result.

I'm sure that there are people that you spend time with that give you access to moments without needing a facade. They allow you to be authentically yourself. Isn't it wonderful? Aren't they the best times and your best people?

I invite you to drop the act, permanently. Relax your shoulders, breathe out and accept everything you are. It's beautiful. It's you. It's unique and you suit some people perfectly. Trying to become someone else for the sake of others is just a complete waste of time and energy.

It's time to reintroduce yourself. But first, let's become really clear on who you are. Again, this is not who you want to be or who people think you are. It's who you are naturally, authentically and who you can most confidently be. Here are some thoughts to allow yourself to emerge.

> **You've always been you.** You don't need to reinvent. You just need to rediscover. Once, you were confident. You had fun too, and you didn't see anything wrong with doing something for no better reason than the sheer joy of it. Somewhere along the way, you have forgotten how to do those things and the personality that goes with them. The techniques in this book aren't intended to turn you into a different person. They will allow you to rediscover the fun, confident person you once were.
>
> **You don't need other people's permission to be you.** You are unique. You have a combination of skills, abilities and experience shared by no-one else. You are driven by your own individual values, aspirations and dreams. You do not exist only as a reflection of other people's perceptions. If

you were the only person in the world, you'd still be you. You cannot be what everyone else wants and you cannot be liked by everyone. Accept that and instead, give yourself permission to be you. Living your own life confidently, according to your own values and while having fun, makes you a more interesting and attractive person and a stronger friend, parent, partner, and colleague. Unleashing the real you will inspire, help and support the people around you.

Remember who you are. Some people are so lacking in confidence and so concerned with seeking approval from others that they forget who they really are. They try to be everything to everyone and end up being nothing at all. The story of you isn't intended for other people: it's about and for you. You are a fascinating person worthy of respect and love. To reveal your real qualities, you need to get back in touch with your own core values. You need to do things because you enjoy them, not because other people expect you to do them. You need to allow your own personality to emerge and to remember how to speak naturally and to act in ways that are meaningful to you. You need to remember how to be you.

Choose the best parts. You have skills, talents and experience that mean you are good at some things. You are probably really great at a few things. In other parts of your life, you may struggle. Don't waste time beating yourself up about those. Know where you excel and focus your time and energy on those areas. Some of your friends, family and colleagues provide you with support and encouragement. Some don't. Make a conscious effort to spend more time with people who will increase your self-confidence. Ensure that you are a positive and supportive friend, partner, family member and colleague.

Act! Learning and acquiring new ideas provides a wonderful foundation for any life change. But that change will only happen when you take action by using that information. It's too easy to become so immersed in research and learning that this actually delays taking action. It's tempting to avoid discomfort by staying with the familiar and within existing routines. Don't let that happen to you. Action leads to uncertainty and facing up to the possibility of failure. But only action leads to positive change. Be prepared to act!

Use these five headings to think about your true identity. What do you like? Who do you like? What are you good at? What do you want to spend your time on?

If you adopted this identity and allowed it to guide you and your behavior, how would your life change? If someone meets you again in 12 months, how will your life be different?

In your Workbook is an exercise which will ignite your freedom to be whoever you truly are. Stop now and do that exercise. It will be impactful.

In the next part of this book, we will show you what actions you need to take. These are proven, practical techniques you can use to restore your self-confidence and to fundamentally enhance your life.

PART 3

Powerful New Things To Do

12

LESS TALK. MORE WALK

The Easiest Way To Instantly Become Relevant

If you always do what you've always done, you'll always get what you always got.

– James P. Lewis

You dream of a great life. You want satisfying relationships, enough money, and fulfillment in what you do. There are just two ways of achieving those things. You can wait for luck, chance, or a beneficent deity to provide them. Or you can get out there and make them happen.

It's certainly possible that the first approach will make you rich and happy. Just doing what you have always done and dreaming about change <u>might</u> bring you what you want. However, it probably won't. If you're happy to leave your destiny to chance, I wish you all the luck in the world.

However, if you're more inclined to take matters into your own hands, let's talk not about relying on luck and how you can take charge of your own future. If you're reading this book, you want to change your life. In Chapter 8 we talked about the importance of taking action in making change happen. That's so critical that I want to come back to it here.

> **Action makes knowledge real.** Knowledge and learning are wonderful things. Without them you won't get far. But action makes both knowledge and learning real. Suppose you are thinking about starting your own business. That's one of the most common dreams for people who feel trapped in the nine-to-five grind. Many people read everything they can about starting their own business. But some use this simply as fuel for dreams. It's only when you use that knowledge as the basis for action that it becomes real. Then, you can really understand how that information fits <u>your</u> life, <u>your</u> circumstances, <u>your</u> passions, and <u>your</u> strengths. That refines the knowledge to the point that it

becomes truly useful. If you just think about things, you will endlessly repeat the same loop. The feedback that comes only from taking action is vital for informing the next action. Knowledge + Action = Success. Success + Learning = More effective action. Taking action ignites a chain-reaction that leads to positive life change.

Self-help means helping yourself. This is a self-help book. You already knew that, right? Do you know why most self-help books don't actually help people to make positive changes? It's not because the books are necessarily bad, it's because people don't use the knowledge they take from them as the basis for action. All the knowledge in the world won't make one ounce of difference to your life unless you back it up with action. Reading this book cannot change your life. Taking action using the techniques in this book will.

Action conquers fear. Taking action means facing uncertainty. You may be doing something you have never done before. That's scary. In fact, fear of the unknown is the single most common reason that people don't take action. But every time you act, whether you're successful or not, you learn. Learning reduces uncertainty and that reduces fear.

Action builds momentum. Inertia is one of the hardest things to overcome. It can feel like you are trying to move a huge boulder. But once it starts moving, it immediately gets easier. It takes less effort to keep it rolling. Any action, no matter how small, helps to maintain momentum. And once you have that boulder rolling, nothing will stop you!

Action makes you confident. This is a book about building your self-confidence. Increasing your self-confidence will only happen when you act. If you allow uncertainty and fear to block you from taking action, you will never become self-confident. If you act, you <u>will</u> become more self-confident.

Only action leads to change. If you already have a perfect life, then there's no need to change. You're done. Congratulations. For everyone else, change is good. Change leads to improvement. But thinking about change and talking about it won't make a difference. Only action will lead to real change.

You get the picture. If you aren't willing to take action, you're doomed to repeat the same, tired loop forever. When I was a young man, I really, really wanted to become a motorcycle racer. I was a pretty good road rider and I could easily picture myself as the next Barry Sheene. I bought an old race bike and spent two seasons racing. I was dreadful. When I wasn't bringing up the rear of the pack I was face down with a mouthful of gravel. I discovered that the skills a racer needs are quite different and I learned that I just didn't have them. The only trophies I got during my brief racing career were additions to my already impressive scar collection.

Was that a complete waste of my time then? Emphatically no! If I hadn't tried it, I'd probably still have frustrating dreams about being a racer. I learned that wasn't for me. Instead, I pursued things that I had natural skills in. Things that were incredibly fulfilling and satisfying. Things I would probably never have tried if I hadn't first scratched that racing itch. Taking action leads to learning. That may send you off in an unexpected direction, but it's much, much better than standing still.

There are also some less tangible benefits that taking action brings. One of the most notable is respect. If you take action to achieve your goals, that sends out a message of commitment and willingness that commands respect.

Here's what I want you to do:

> **Stop talking about it.** Do you know anyone who talks about what they're going to do and never actually does it? I do and I hate it. You probably do too. I have one friend, Greg, who's a great guy. But he has kind of a thing about motorcycles. He has watched every episode of *Long Way Round* and *Long Way Down* and read more books than I can count about making great motorcycle journeys. He knows the best routes through Turkmenistan and can speak at length of the relative merits of the BMW GS1200 and the F750GS. But he doesn't own a motorcycle or even have a motorcycle license. I have tried to encourage him to buy a small bike and take some lessons, but he'd rather talk about crossing the Sahara. He won't take even the smallest first step towards actually doing any of the things he talks about. I think he's afraid that riding around on a small bike while wearing a dayglo vest will puncture his dreams of traveling the world. He doesn't see that the only way of achieving those dreams is to take that first step. He'd rather just talk about it. I get bored listening to Greg. Don't be like him. No-one will be impressed when

you just talk about something. Do it first, then talk about it. Then they will be impressed.

Stop thinking about it. You already have all the knowledge you need. More knowledge won't increase your chances of success. It's possible to become lost within a quest for knowledge. The only thing you need now is the learning that comes from taking action. The rest is just more useless stuff filling the inside of your head.

Look at the people around you. Do the people you spend time with take action? Or do they just sit around talking about it? Make a conscious effort to hang out with people who are willing to act and let them inspire you to do the same.

Do it! When is the perfect time to take action? Maybe next month, when you're not so busy? Or next summer, when the weather's better? Perhaps it might be best to wait until you retire: you'll have lots of time then. None of these answers are right. Life is slipping by, day-by-day, minute-by-minute. This isn't a rehearsal. This is all you get. If you want to change your life for the better, you have to act. Now.

Open your Workbook and take the steps in there. They will transform your relationship with action.

It doesn't really matter what you do. You may even find yourself heading in the wrong direction, but that will just give you a clearer idea of where the right direction is. You can start in a very small way, as long as you get that boulder rolling. But here's a thought: you could instead do something massive. You could do something inspirational and important. You could make a genuine difference. How does that sound? In the next Chapter, we'll be talking about doing big things.

13

DO
BIG
THINGS

How To Get Instant Inspiration

You will spend the same amount of time and energy on whatever you choose to do, so make sure it's BIG. BIG is where all the fun is.

– Kevin Abdulrahman

A very smart guy (it was economist E. F. Schumacher, as you ask) once said: "*Small is beautiful*". He was really talking about the use of resources, and in that, he's certainly right. Some other things are also much better small. Spiders, hurdles, pills. But small isn't intrinsically good. Sometimes, big is just so much better.

Suppose that you are interested in charity. That's great and it's a positive way to make a difference. You can do it small by simply setting up a standing order to donate a certain amount to the charity of your choice every month. There is nothing wrong with that, but you could also do it big. You could set up your own charitable organization to target a particular disadvantaged group. You could put your feet on the ground, actually spending time helping those people.

Which of those two approaches is inspirational? If you met two people, one who made a monthly donation to a charity and one who spent time working in an orphanage in a third-world country, who would you rather talk with? Which of these people would you give the most respect and admiration? Which of those people would you rather be?

In the last Chapter's Workbook exercise we saw your amazing capacity for action. In this Chapter, I want to ask you to open the throttle a little. Consider big things when you're planning any action. Big things make a big difference, to you as well as to others.

When you're thinking about the big thing you'd like to achieve, think about the thing that would bring you the most joy. Think about why you would want to achieve this and what difference it would make to your life and to other people. It doesn't have to be altruistic, like doing charity work. It might be that you want to run the company you now work for or even start your own company.

It might be that you want to travel the world, or change the world or your big thing might be to create a stunning relationship with your kids, your family or partner. It might be that you want to start a band. The element that really distinguishes big things from little things is that big things take more time to achieve.

Big things are generally done by doing a string of smaller things in succession. Your goal may be huge, but if you can break that down into manageable chunks, it will be easier to make progress. Think about the sub-goals and milestones that move you towards achieving that big thing. You want to start a band? Well, maybe you'll begin by getting out there and meeting people who want to join you. It probably means practicing more too!

Think about why you want to do this big thing? Specifically, what is it that you want to achieve? Don't just say: *I want to give to charity*. Instead: *I want to build a school in Cambodia*. Don't say: *I want to be happy*. Rather: *I want to be in a fulfilling marriage and to have 2 children*. The more specific you can be, the easier it will be to identify the steps you have to take to get there.

Once you know where you want to be and you know what you need to do, it's easy: you just keep going until you're done. Along the way, you'll discover that you have conquered your own fear and self-doubt. I know that you can achieve big things. All you have to do is decide what they are.

Achieving big things brings joy and emotional satisfaction. That helps to maintain your motivation when the going gets hard. Big things also inspire other people. They will command respect from others who may even want to become involved. But remember that big things are achieved by completing a string of smaller things. In the next Chapter we'll look at those little things.

14

DO LITTLE THINGS

A Guaranteed Method For High Self-Esteem

Great things are done by a series of small things brought together.

– Vincent Van Gogh

Big things command attention. People love to be involved in a big vision. Big things draw bigger and better resources and talent. Big things are inspiring. Big things often take just as much energy as less significant things and doing big things can provide a huge boost to your self-confidence.

However, most people don't have a proper sense of what 'big' means. Big can seem overwhelming and, as such, it's often where people withdraw. However, big is just a lot of little things done with one consistent objective in mind.

And, for big things to happen, one must do the little things. Most people lose sight of the overall objective when they're doing the paperwork or the cleaning or trying to gather support in the early stages of a project or dealing with a tiny group of followers. Most people don't have the foresight or the persistence to continue doing the small things long enough for the big, scary, inspiring goal to be realized.

I urge you to change. Don't be like most. Please, for the sake of your goals and all the amazing things that you could do in this world and all the people relying on you to do them, change.

Adopt the view that small is good. Small is rewarding. Small is noble, humble and necessary. Nothing good was created in haste. Be patient. It will happen. There's only one thing you have to avoid at all costs – stopping. Don't stop. Continue to do the small things well after everyone else has gone home. Stay back. Find the energy. Do one more. And then do the same thing tomorrow.

What small things should I do? Great question! There's another important ingredient in the achievement of big things that is not common to many people – discrimination.

Small things can provide a safe place to hide. They're low risk and often low cost. Some folks will spend a lot of time on the small stuff and pretend to be making progress. The antidote to this busy, unproductive cycle is to discriminate between what's critical and what's optional.

It's a shift in your mind that's needed at the start of the journey towards anything significant and it begins with the obvious question:

Is this critical?

If there are 100 things to do, maybe 10 of them will be critical. Critical means that if these things are not done, it will not be possible to achieve the goal. Optional just means that it could be done but it has no direct bearing on whether you achieve your goal.

For example, starting an online business could include purchasing stationery, registering a business name, creating a logo, buying a domain name, sourcing a supplier, hiring a bookkeeper, buying a new desk, hosting a launch party, hiring an assistant.

Only a few of those things are critical. It takes an enormous amount of discipline to resist the temptation to do those things that may be fun and would make you feel busy but are not critical to achieving your outcome.

So, here is the new way of thinking that guarantees you'll make 'big' possible.

- Know that big is just lots of small things lined up in a row
- Know that big success relies on you distinguishing critical from optional
- To get big, start small and don't stop.

There are now some important actions to take in your Workbook. Stop here and get those done. You'll commence the creation of some amazing plans.

As you plan and work towards your inspiring goals, share them on the LearnWell Community. Inspiring others is a rewarding way to gain confidence in your ideas. However, it's also important to adopt a  practice of acceptance. It's a critical tool in restoring your self-confidence. That's what we'll be covering in the next Chapter.

15

I ACCEPT THIS.
ALL OF IT.
EVEN THE BAD BITS

The Fastest Way To Peace

What you resist, persists.

– Carl Jung

Suppose two people you know well were meeting for the first time. You'd probably be happy to give each a brief summary of the other person in a couple of sentences: *"Nice woman. Gentle and kind. Never mean. Fun. Likes cats. Totally into movies."* You'd do it easily. You probably wouldn't have to spend much time thinking about it because you already have a short bio of everyone you know inside your head. But could you do the same for yourself?

That's way harder, isn't it? Partly of course it's because you know yourself better than anyone else. But negativity bias also means that you are acutely aware of your own perceived failures and failings than those of other people. You would probably be much more negative in summing yourself up than you would anyone else. Those negative feelings can undermine your efforts to increase self-confidence. In this Chapter we're going to take a look at that and provide some tips for changing the way you think about yourself by using something called acceptance.

Imagine that you come out of your house one morning ready to get into your car and drive to work. Then, you notice that you have a flat tire. It would be strange if you didn't feel a surge of irritation, maybe even anger at that point. Life has just thrown you an unexpected curve-ball. How you react after that tells you a great deal about yourself. If you spend the rest of the day in a state of irritation, if you have the feeling that *"life's just not fair!,"* then that's a problem. I'm amazed at how many people I meet who seem to have the feeling that life is somehow out to get them.

Life is neither fair nor unfair. It is what it is. Sometimes it includes punctures. Sometimes it doesn't. You can't change those things. What you can change is your own reaction. If you allow a flat tire to leave you feeling grouchy for the rest of the day, if it makes you rude to other people, angry and exasperated, that minor problem will define your day. You'll have a bad day. If you are able to practice acceptance, after your initial surprise and irritation, you will think: *"OK, I have a flat. What do I need to do to get it fixed and get to work?"* You will get over it, move on and still have the option to have a good day.

Acceptance isn't about resignation or being defeatist. It moves you out of victim mode and recognizes that the most effective way to deal with anything is to accept the emotions it brings and then move on. Acceptance doesn't mean not trying to change or giving up on improving. It means accepting that you are where you are now and using that as the basis for deciding what to do next. Acceptance can apply to so many other aspects of your life.

> **Accept your past.** Sometimes, remembering things I have done in the past can cause such an acute twinge of emotional pain that I wince. Usually when I'm remembering occasions when I have behaved like a complete asshole. I know, you find it hard to believe that a calm, self-aware guy like me can act and feel that way but, trust me here, it's true. There are times in the past when I haven't behaved well. But what I have learned to accept is that I can't change those things. I cannot go back and do them over. All I can do is to try to behave better in the present.
>
> Guilt, shame, and regret are some of the most pointless and destructive emotions you can feel. They're about the past, which you cannot change. If you allow yourself to dwell on those feelings, they will undermine your

self-confidence and make you feel lousy about yourself. Instead, recognize that those feelings tell you where you have behaved in ways that don't mesh with your values. Instead of beating yourself up about the past, think about how the learning that comes from that would make you act differently now. We all make mistakes. We all have failures. You must learn to accept those things, to understand what they have taught you and to move on. If you can't learn to accept it, the past can define the present.

Accept other people. You cannot change other people. That's a fundamental fact that so many people seem to forget. It is within your power to change yourself. Other people have the same power, but they must choose to use it. You can offer advice and guidance if those things are asked for, but that's all you can do.

If you can't learn to accept other people, you will never truly learn to love. If you are in love with what you think another person should be or might become, that's only ever going to lead to disappointment and frustration for both of you. The best relationships are those where both people accept the other. No-one is perfect. We all have faults. Even me. Those things are part of what makes us ourselves. You can choose to be in a relationship with someone or not to be. That's all that lies within your power. Accept that and deal with the relationships you have, not some fantasy of the relationship you'd like.

Accept yourself. This is the big one. Everything starts with this. Of course, you can learn and grow and improve. But you're still going to be you. What goes on inside your head defines how you interact with the world. If you are angry with yourself, you're going to be angry with other people. If you are disappointed with yourself, you are going to be disappointed with everyone else. The failings we see in others are often just reflections of our own failings.

When I was at school, I had a good friend. He was smart and funny, but he seemed to have real problems relating to others, especially girls. It was only much later in life that he admitted to me that he was very self-conscious about his ears. He felt that they stuck out too much, which made him feel that everyone was looking at him. At first, I thought he was kidding. I might even have laughed until I realized that he was serious. I guess maybe his ears did stick out a bit, but I had never really noticed or thought about it.

It was only after a few beers one evening that he admitted that he found it very difficult to talk to people because he thought that they must be looking at his ears. In addition, when he first met someone, the first thing he looked at was their ears: did they stick out? If they did, he tended to avoid that person. Underlying that was the assumption that no-one would want to spend time with a person whose ears stuck out. He was so wrapped up in his own skewed self-perception that it defined how he looked at the world.

My friend was an extreme example. And, just for the record, he did get over it. He thought about getting his ears fixed, but eventually came to see that maybe how far his ears stuck out didn't define how the world saw him. He learned that he had other qualities that made him likable and even loveable. He learned acceptance. Lots of us have flawed self-perception that leads us to misperceive how the world sees us. We may exaggerate our own flaws way beyond what other people see. We may project those perceptions onto other people. These may be about our physical appearance or some aspect of our personality. We can only move on from that by beginning with acceptance. You are what you are. If your ears stick out, live with it. You cannot be self-confident until you learn to accept yourself.

AFFIRMATION

There is a technique you can use to increase your ability for acceptance and especially acceptance of yourself. It's called affirmation and it simply means repeating positive statements to yourself regularly.

Stop! I know that you're thinking of flipping to the next page, looking for some good, practical advice and not this woo-woo stuff. I know what you're thinking because I felt that way too when I first heard about affirmation. Just hang on a moment and let me explain.

Words are incredibly powerful. Words shape your conception of the world and your perception of your place in it. Words define you and everything you do. Back in 1988, American psychologist Claude Steele proposed something called *Self-Affirmation Theory*[25]. He explained that self-image and self-confidence can be improved simply by speaking positive affirmations.

Finding the words to describe a positive situation isn't just wishful thinking. If you repeat these words often enough, evidence suggests that they actually rewire your brain and make it easier to deal with stress and to establish and continue behaviors that will bring about that situation[26]. In simple terms, affirmations are positive phrases or statements that challenge negative thoughts, support positive change, provide motivation, and boost self-confidence. You repeat these affirmations to yourself every day and this produces changes in your brain. This isn't magic. It's a widely accepted psychological approach that really works.

What phrases or statements should you use? They will be unique to your situation and your aspirations. They will reflect where you are now and where you want to be. They can cover anything you want (and you'll find more detailed guidance on affirmations in the Workbook) but they might include things like:

- I control my life.
- I have everything I need to succeed.
- I choose to be content.
- I choose to be positive.
- I can attain the future I plan.
- I am filled with health and energy.
- Every day, I learn and grow.
- Today will be a great day.
- Each day, I make progress towards my goals.

You may feel deeply suspicious of affirmation. I certainly was initially. How can just repeating positive things make them happen? Saying these things to yourself every day can't change the world. But it can change the way in which you think about the world and it can increase your capacity for acceptance. Using affirmations won't stop you getting a flat tire. But it will allow you to encounter such a challenge constructively instead of allowing it to spoil your whole day. Build affirmations into your daily routine. It will make a greater difference than you might believe.

Using affirmations won't stop you failing either. And failure is something that you need to accept too. As you strive for improvement, you *will* experience failure along the way. That failure is less important than how you deal with it, and that's what we'll be looking at in the next Chapter.

16

KEEP GETTING UP

The One Ingredient In Life That Ultimately Determines Success

*You may encounter many defeats,
but you must not be defeated.*

– Maya Angelou

You're going to fail. If you're reading this book, you're most likely human. And humans are flawed. They make mistakes. Sometimes they fail. You will too. What you have to understand is that failure isn't the end of the story. In fact, it may be an essential step on the ultimate road to success.

I wrote my first book many, many years ago. I had a full-time day job, but I hated it. What I really wanted to be was a writer. I invested months of evenings and weekends crouched over an early word-processor. I drank too much coffee. I smoked a lot back then too and spent too much time surrounded by overflowing ashtrays. Finally, it was done. Proudly I sent it out to as many potential publishers as I could find. I sat back and waited confidently for an avalanche of offers. I got just one reply. It noted that the manuscript "*could have been funnier.*"

I was devastated. I had been confident that the book could have been a best-seller. I put it aside for a couple of years, came back to it and made a few revisions. I sent it out again to a different group of publishers. This time, I didn't get a single reply. That hurt a lot. I had poured everything into it and no-one wanted to read it. Failing to find a publisher and then failing to sell on Amazon felt like the end of the world.

It's only now, with the perspective that time brings, that I can see that I wasn't actually very good as a writer back then. I hadn't learned enough about the craft to write a full-length book. However, the experience of writing that book led me to look for other part-time writing work. I produced articles for magazines and, when the Internet came along, for web sites. Now, I'm a full-time professional writer. FYI, it's the best job in the world. I can do it on the beach. I can do it in a bar or coffee shop. I can do it in the middle of the night in my pajamas if that's what I want. Every book I write, I learn a little more about being a writer and the topic I'm writing about. While by any objective standard, that first book I wrote was a failure, it began a path that led directly to where I am today. If I hadn't written that first unsuccessful book, I wonder whether I would ever have become a full-time writer?

Everybody who strives to achieve something risks failure. Failure should not be seen as necessarily bad. Perhaps we should even see it as a rite of passage? Show me someone who has never failed and I'll show you someone who has never tried. But how and why you fail matter.

If you reflect on things in your life that you regard as failures, I think you'll see that many of them happened because you simply gave up. You worked towards getting fitter but you stopped going to the gym. You started eating healthily but you went back to burgers and take-out food. You stopped smoking but then you started again. You only failed because you lacked persistence.

~~Don't do that again!~~

There _are_ sometimes good reasons for quitting (and we'll be talking more about those in a moment) but just keeping on is a powerful way to overcome obstacles. Imagine if you hadn't given up on those things. How would your life be different today? How different would my life have been if I had given up writing after the failure of my first book? When you're tempted to give up on anything, here are few things to remember:

Stay focused on your goals. The things that you invest time and energy in should move you towards your goals. If they don't, why are you spending time on them? Staying focused on those goals and celebrating every tiny piece of progress keeps you motivated and encourages you to keep going.

It's going to take time. Achieving anything useful takes time. That's a pain, but it's just how life works. The more effort you have to put in, the more worthwhile the outcome. You can't sustainably lose weight in two weeks. You can't quickly gain the skills and knowledge you need to change your career. If something is important to you, you're probably going to need to do it for some time. Understand and accept that when you start.

Keep going! If you plant a seed, there is no point standing over it and waiting for something to happen. No matter how impatient you are, it isn't going to grow any faster. It's the same with almost anything you do. If you keep investing time and effort, you <u>will</u> see results. If you give up, you'll never see that seed grow into something beautiful.

If it was easy, everyone would be doing it. This was one of my father's favorite sayings. I got kind of tired of hearing it, but it happens to be true. If you're doing something and it seems easy, that probably means lots of other people would find it easy too. If you're doing something and you find it tough, the same thing applies. If you can keep going even when it is difficult, you are more likely to achieve something unique, worthwhile and truly useful.

Even if you don't give up, not everything you do will succeed. You really need to understand and accept that. Don't allow failures to undermine your self-confidence. Instead, take them as a measure of your ambition and desire for change. If you have the courage to try something different, you may fail. Provided that you learn from that and invest your amazing abilities and talents in something different, you are still making progress.

MAYBE IT IS TIME TO QUIT?

Persistence is a great quality. The ability to pick yourself up and keep going is the route to achieving your goals. But persistence does not mean never quitting. If you take people like Thomas Edison or James Dyson, who are often cited as examples of the benefits of persistence, you will see that each actually quit many times. They quit working on something that wasn't going to deliver and switched to something that might.

Quitting because you're tired, or it all seems like too much work or because you are nervous is never good. Quitting because you aren't getting any closer to your goals or because you believe that the effort required isn't justified by the potential benefits can actually be a good idea. You only have so much time and energy. You need to direct them where they will deliver the most benefit. In business, this is called *Smart Quitting*.

Sometimes, *Smart Quitting*, quitting for the right reasons, is the best way forward. Until you try something new, you don't know how it will work out. If you can objectively see that you aren't heading in the right direction, perhaps it is time to quit? Accept that, review what you have learned and move on. Persistence is a positive quality, but unless it's tempered with flexibility and objectivity it can become simple stubbornness. That can lead to a waste of time and energy. Quitting something in which you have an emotional investment is tough. But you don't have to feel embarrassment or guilt about that because sometimes, it's the right choice. Provided that you learn from it, quitting can refocus you on a more direct route to your goals.

<u>Have you failed yet?</u> If not, maybe you aren't making enough effort to change your life? Failure is an inevitable part of making progress. Don't hide from it and don't beat yourself up. Accept, learn, and move on. Every failure means you get a little better at what you do. Don't try to hide your failures from other people. Talk about them, about what they mean to you and what you learned. Fortunately, one of the things that becoming self-confident will allow you to do is to talk to people in more effective and meaningful ways. That's what we're going to be discussing in the next Chapter.

17

BE THE LION AND ROAR!

How To Use Life-Changing Communication

To be passive is to let others decide for you.
To be aggressive is to decide for others.
To be assertive is to decide for yourself.

– Edith Eva Eger

I want to try a word-association test here. If I say "*assertiveness*," what word or words spring to mind for you? I imagine that you may have chosen words like "*arrogant*," "*aggressive*," "*selfish*," or even "*bullying*." Incorrect Assertiveness isn't about trying to dominate other people. In fact, learning to communicate with confident assertion is one of the most useful skills you can learn and an essential step on the road towards self-confidence.

Assertiveness is a communication skill. It involves learning how to say what's important to you without ignoring the needs of others. That's the difference between, for example, assertiveness and arrogance: arrogance means simply backing your own views while ignoring those of everyone else. Assertiveness is applicable to every aspect of your life, including your career, friendships and relationships. Becoming assertive doesn't mean that you will always get your own way but it will significantly boost your self-confidence.

SAYING "*YES*" WHEN YOU WANT TO SAY "*NO*"

People who lack self-confidence find one word more difficult than any other: *no*. We all want to be liked. When someone asks us for something or to do something, we're pre-programmed to say: *yes*. That makes us feel valued and wanted. It avoids potential confrontation. We're afraid that saying *no* will make the other person like us less.

Here's the problem: every time you say *yes* when you really want to say *no*, you're reducing your self-esteem and eating into the time and energy you have available for pursuing your own goals.

You are likely to increase your feelings of resentment and that's not good for any relationship.

Sometimes, we even lie to avoid saying *no*. Perhaps someone asks you to look after their dog for a couple of days. Instead of honestly saying that you're working on several projects and just don't have the time to walk a dog two or three times each day, you instead claim that you're going away for the weekend. That's not good on several levels. One, you're not being honest and that's not good for any relationship. Two, if someone sees you during the weekend and tells that person, they're going to know that you were lying. That will hurt the relationship even more. Finally, you will get irritated by your own gutlessness: why didn't you just say *no*? That undermines your confidence.

There is no way around it: if you want to be confident, you must be able to see when you really want to say *yes* and otherwise say *no*. American writer Derek Sivers[27] has described a great way of deciding when to say yes. If your response is a totally enthusiastic "*Hell Yeah!*" then you should say *yes*. To everything else, you should say *no*.

There are probably relatively few requests or offers to which you will respond with "*Hell Yeah!*" Which means you're going to be saying *no* a lot more. That's not a bad thing. Some other people may have a problem with it, particularly if they're used to you always saying *yes*. Some may even spend less time with you when you learn to say *no*. I'm afraid you'll have to deal with that. Remind yourself that if people only liked you because you were always willing to say *yes*, perhaps they weren't people you really want to spend time with?

Learning to say *no* is liberating and empowering. It boosts your self-confidence and makes you appreciate how often you say *yes* when you don't really mean it. Make saying *no* part of your everyday life at work, at home and everywhere else. However, sometimes you need to go further than a simple no when you want to assert yourself.

ASSERTING YOURSELF

Asserting yourself generally involves describing clearly a situation or behavior that's making you unhappy. Fortunately, there is a great technique for doing this: it's called the three-part assertion message. The three parts are:

- Describe the problem.
- Say how the problem makes you feel.
- A clarification of how the problem affects you.

The most effective assertion messages are short, with all three elements combined in a single sentence. For example, you might use the following assertiveness message to deal with a problem behavior:

 When you leave your stuff lying around, I feel stressed because I have to tidy-up when I get back from work.

For a workplace issue:

 Working on this project makes me feel stressed because I don't have sufficient staff.

These messages are a great way of learning to assert your feelings. They're also simple, which makes them easy for another person to understand. But you'll notice that something seems to be missing here: the solution. That's deliberate. Remember, you can only change yourself, not other people. If, for example, someone's crude jokes are making you feel bad, simply telling them to stop probably won't work. If instead you tell them how that makes you feel, you're leaving them free to change their behavior to create the solution.

If you find yourself in a situation where an assertion message would be helpful, take the time to write down a three-part message and to rehearse saying it. The first time you do this will probably feel challenging, but each time you do it, it will get easier. If you lack confidence, you aren't used to asserting what you want. This is a key skill to learn and use.

Pick your time and then just give your three-part assertion message and wait. Don't be tempted to apologize or justify: you have an absolute right to say how you feel. Be prepared to repeat the message until the person or people you're talking to begin to suggest solutions. Engage with that process and continue until you arrive at a solution that has the potential to make you happy. If the other person seems completely unwilling to suggest a solution, you can't force them. However, you can make a choice not to spend time with that person.

Spend some time with your Workbook and explore some very interesting new ideas about your new assertive character.

Becoming assertive takes time. Learning how to say no and how to assert your needs can feel scary. But trust me, these things will make an incredible difference to your self-confidence. Once you discover your ability to clearly express your true needs in personal and professional relationships, it will, literally change your life!

One of the things that learning to be assertive will do is to help you establish and protect your personal boundaries. These are the invisible web of emotional and physical limits that define what you will and won't do. They're fundamental to your sense of wellbeing but no-one else can see them. What are you going to do about that? That's what we'll be talking about in the next Chapter.

18

THIS IS MY SPACE

How To Set Boundaries That Create Control And Confidence

Daring to set boundaries is about having the courage to love ourselves.

– Bren Brown

Imagine that a stranger approaches you. They get closer and closer and suddenly, when they get within a certain distance, you will begin to feel very uncomfortable indeed. The reason for your discomfort is that the other person has crossed a personal boundary. They have entered a physical area that you regard as your personal space. Every person has their own concept of how large this personal space is and everyone feels uncomfortable if that is ignored.

But it isn't just physical space that we protect with boundaries. We have emotional boundaries too which, if crossed, also make us feel uncomfortable. The problem with these personal boundaries is that they aren't marked on any map or defined by flags and fences. They exist only inside our heads and they are different for each of us. That doesn't mean that they aren't important but it does mean that other people can cross them without realizing. To be confident, you must learn to clearly set out and protect your own personal boundaries.

Boundaries come into play virtually every time you have any form of interaction with another person. They can be physical: defining an imaginary space inside which you do not want another person to enter uninvited or physical contact such as hugging or kissing. They may be emotional: there may be topics you are not comfortable talking about or listening to others talk about. They may be material: you may feel a need to protect your belongings or your property. They may be about time: you may want to protect your time within a crowded schedule.

For me, I just don't like being touched unless it's by someone with whom I have an intimate relationship. Sitting next to someone who punctuates what they're saying by continually clutching my arm or touching my hand makes me wince. I know that isn't logical and that some people like physical contact as part of casual conversation. They don't mean me any harm, but it makes me feel uncomfortable. If I find myself next to someone like that, I tend to unconsciously shuffle away from them. They tend to follow so they can continue to touch me. It ends up like an absurd dance where I back off and they try to close the distance.

It took me a long time to recognize this in myself and to see that it was causing problems. There were people I liked, who I often really enjoyed talking to. But their touchy-feely approach made me back-off. That's just plain stupid. But it isn't uncommon. Because there are three critical things that you need to remember about these boundaries:

- Every person has a unique and different set of personal boundaries.
- It isn't possible for another person to guess what your boundaries are.
- You have the absolute right to assert and protect your own personal boundaries.

That's the heart of the problem. You (and everyone else) are surrounded by an invisible web of emotional and physical boundaries. These vary from person to person and culture to culture. No-one else can see them but if these boundaries are crossed, you'll feel uncomfortable. You want to avoid that, so what can you do?

You have to tell people what your personal boundaries are.

I have come to recognize that it really is that simple. If you want people to respect your personal boundaries, you first have to communicate just what they are. That can seem scary. It can make you feel nervous. But if you don't do it, your relationships will suffer as people inadvertently trample over your boundaries without realizing why you're becoming unhappy.

Fortunately, you can also use the three-part assertiveness messages described in the last Chapter to help define your boundaries. For example, to describe an emotional boundary you could use:

> *When you make sexist jokes, I feel really uncomfortable because I detest sexism.*

For defining a physical boundary, you might say:

> *When you hug me, I don't feel good because I don't like being touched by people I don't know well.*

For a property boundary, you could use:

> *When you use my mug, I feel uncomfortable because I don't like drinking from the same mug as someone else.*

For a time boundary, you could say:

> *When you spend half an hour talking about television shows, I feel stressed because there are lots of other things I need to be doing.*

The great thing about these three-part messages is that they can be adapted to any situation and to describe any kind of boundary. Just as with any other type of assertiveness message, don't be tempted to apologize or justify. Your boundaries may be different to those of others. That's just part of your personality. They matter to you and you have the right to explain what they are. By describing these you aren't violating another person's boundaries or rights, you are simply asserting your own.

When you have given this type of message, the rest is up to the other person. Hopefully, they will choose to respect the boundary you have described. If they continue to violate your boundaries, you can try repeating the three-part message. If that doesn't work, you have the right to create further space between yourself and that person. If they persist, you may choose not to spend time with them at all.

What I invite you to accept is that your personal boundaries matter. If you try to ignore them, you're going to spend a great deal of time feeling bad. That's not good for your well being or your self-confidence. It also makes it difficult for you to establish meaningful relationships. Defining these boundaries won't make you less likable. It will help other people by understanding what makes you feel uncomfortable and what your limits are. Defining these will also help you to feel more confident and better about yourself. How you feel about yourself is important and it's something we'll be talking about in detail in the next Chapter.

19

I LOVE ME SO MUCH!

Ways Of Showing Love To The Most Lovable Person In The World

"Today you are you! That is truer than true! There is no one alive who is you-er than you!"

– Dr Seuss

Loving yourself is another exercise in acceptance. You know yourself better than you know anyone else. You are acutely aware of your own failings as well as your strengths. But when you learn to accept those things, you are better able to improve the most important relationship you will ever have: your relationship with yourself.

Hang on. Stay with me I can hear you say that people who love themselves are arrogant and bumptious and insufferable, aren't they? You really don't want to turn yourself into someone like that! Let's see if we can understand what's really going on here and why the root of real confidence is self-love.

We all know people who like to boast. About their accomplishments, their belongings and even their physical prowess. You know the kind of people I mean. Anything you talk about, they have already done better, they have a bigger one, or they have bought a more expensive one. On the surface, they might seem supremely confident. Underneath, they really aren't. Anyone who feels the need to constantly assert their own superiority only does that because they don't really believe in it.

That's just a fundamental fact of life. It may not be immediately obvious, but people who boast are insecure. People who boast a lot are very insecure. I have an acquaintance who has a thing about watches. Every time we meet, he seems to have a new one. He doesn't seem to have any issue with spending several thousand dollars on a watch. Whenever I meet him, one of the first things he does is to show me his new watch and tell me how much it cost. The second thing is usually to mock my watch.

I tend to spend anything up to $15 on my watches. My criteria is simple: it has to keep good time. Plastic straps are preferred because they don't rot or corrode, as I live by the ocean. I have had my current watch for 5 years, and it still works just fine. Clearly, this acquaintance sees watches as representing something else, and I don't think it has much to do with telling the time.

People who truly love and accept themselves don't need to boast. They don't need expensive watches, clothes or cars to make them feel good either. That can make them hard to spot. You may have to think about the people you know carefully. If you know someone who seems confident, content, and comfortable in their own skin, that person likes themselves. They just don't feel the need to tell you that.

If you're going to become self-confident, you're going to have to learn to love and accept yourself. How do you start to do that?

Recognize and reward your achievements. If you're following the guidance in this book, you are growing and learning. You are achieving things you didn't know were possible. It's really important to recognize each step along the way. Did you say no to something you didn't want to do? Give yourself a pat on the back! Did you give a three-part assertion message that defined one of your personal boundaries? Maybe it's time for a little celebration? You deserve it. You're amazing and you're getting even more amazing every day.

Do it regularly. Take the time out every day to think about what you have achieved. Some people find it helpful to make this part of a routine. Maybe as you get into bed and before you settle down to sleep, you should think about what you have achieved during that day? Give yourself a mental pat on the back – you're making progress. Each week, schedule some you-time as a reward. Go for a coffee with a friend, take a walk somewhere beautiful, go to a movie or to a gallery or museum. Whatever works for you. Each month, do something bigger to celebrate your growth. Buy yourself new clothes, take yourself off for the weekend, buy something for your hobby, do something just for the fun of it. Indulge yourself and make that part of your routine.

Spend time with the right people. Back in Chapter 9, we talked about how your relationships help to define how you feel about yourself. Some people make you feel good about yourself. Usually, those are the people who feel good about themselves. Other people seem to do their best to make you feel inadequate and ineffective.. Those people are generally taking out their own lack of self-love on you. I think you already know which type of person you should be spending time with.

In Chapter 15 we talked about how you can use affirmations to boost positive thinking. You can also use these to increase your love for yourself. You just need to use affirmations that are specifically intended to improve how you feel about yourself. For example:

- I accept myself, just as I am.
- I am growing, learning and becoming the best version of myself.

- I accept love from myself.
- I love the person that I am.
- I love my body.
- I am so good at whatever I choose to do.
- I am loveable, inside and out.
- I embrace my uniqueness.
- Everything I need is already inside me.
- I am strong, resilient, and powerful.

Self-love isn't weird or selfish or arrogant. You cannot love anyone else fully until you learn to love yourself. If you quietly think of yourself as weak, flawed, and ineffective, what kind of person is that attracting? How can you truly love someone with judgment so flawed? If you think of yourself as loveable, then someone else's love makes perfect sense. You can respect that person and fully reciprocate their love.

Self-love is a fundamental requirement for self-confidence. However, it's something that exists only inside your own head. Just like the other things you learn about in this book, you don't get a badge, or a certificate, or even a T-shirt once you have achieved self-love. Other people can't see it, but you will know that it's there. It's important that you recognize and accept that separation between physical reality and what you think. Because while you can't control the world outside, you <u>can</u> control what you think. That's what the next the Chapter is about.

20

STOP! DON'T GO THERE

Gaining Control Of The Most Powerful Tool In Confidence Creation

The world is full of magic things, patiently waiting for our senses to grow sharper.

– W.B. Yeats

You experience the world through your five senses. Your brain interprets this information to allow you to perceive what's real. What you see is what you get. Except that's not quite true. There is a wonderful old Indian folk tale that talks about this.

Once, six blind old men lived in a small village. They spent a lot of time gossiping, as old men will. One of the topics they kept returning to was elephants. They had heard a great deal about these animals, but had no idea of what one looked like. Then, an elephant visited the village. The old men were led to it and allowed to touch it so that they could understand better what it was. But each touched only one part of the elephant:

"It's a kind of giant snake,"
said the man who touched the trunk.

"No, it's sharp and dangerous, like a spear,"
said the man who touched the tusk.

"It's just an enormous cow!"
said one who touched a leg.

"It's like a vast carpet,"
said the man who touched an ear.

"It's more like a huge wall,"
said the man who touched the animal's side.

"Pah, it's no more than a piece of old rope!"
said one who tugged on the tail.

Each trusted their senses, but each experienced only one part of the elephant so each had a different and mistaken idea of what the creature looked like. Even when we can see, the relationship between what our senses tell us and how we perceive the world isn't as straightforward as you might think. One neuroscientist Patrick Cavanagh, explains it like this:

> *"It's really important to understand we're not seeing reality. We're seeing a story that's being created for us."* [28]

Why does that matter? Because our perception of the world exists only within our brains. We build a picture of how we think things are based on information from our senses. But just like those old men, we may only see part of the picture and we can then create a false impression. That's a slightly frightening thought, but it has a major positive side: you can't control the world, but you <u>can</u> control your thoughts.

I began thinking about this during my brief career as a motorcycle racer. I could stand in the same place and look at the same scene on two different occasions, yet I would perceive it completely differently. On a bad day, I'd look at the track and see only threats: awkward corners, spilled oil, misplaced barriers, ripples in the tarmac. My thoughts would be entirely concerned with the negative things that could happen. On a good day I'd look at precisely the same vista and see instead opportunities: a place where I knew I could be fast, an opportunity for overtaking, a corner where I could brake a little later than everyone else.

I began to notice that these feelings were self-fulfilling. On bad days I'd ride so defensively and so focused on avoiding problems that I'd perform really badly. Sometimes I'd even fall off on one of the corners I had identified as a potential problem. However, on the good days, I'd do much better. I'd be faster, more confident and more willing and able to use my limited talents to the max.

It was a short step from there to the most important realization of all. In fact, it wouldn't be untrue to say that this was something that changed my life. I came to realize that these varying moods weren't random or inevitable. I could deliberately direct my thoughts to the positive and when I did that, I would perform much better and spend a lot less time picking gravel out from between my teeth.

The way that you think directly affects the way in which you perceive the world and how you perform in it. If you follow negative thoughts and visualize bad things, those things are more likely to happen. If you follow positive thoughts and visualize good things, those are more likely to happen. Crucially, you can decide which to do.

This isn't due to magic or some strange, unexplained force. It's because if you are focused on bad things and potential threats, that's all you'll perceive. The story your brain is telling you is a scary one. You'll miss opportunities and achievements because you just won't see them or you'll regard them as less important than potential threats. Avoiding bad stuff will dominate your thinking and that type of negativity can block you from taking effective action.

You need to be aware of that. If you find yourself locked in a pattern of negative thinking, you <u>must</u> make a conscious effort to change that. If you allow yourself to wallow in regret, fear, and uncertainty, you will never see possible opportunities and you will certainly never become self-confident. There are some good techniques you can use to break the chain of negative thinking:

Affirmations. We have already discussed affirmations as a way of increasing confidence and self-love, but they can also be used to break a cycle of negative thoughts. If you find yourself in that situation, take time out to repeat some of your favorite affirmations. You should find that this helps you get back to a positive outlook. Repeat as often as you need.

Gratitude. Feeling grateful is a wonderful way to combat negativity. We all have things to feel grateful for, whether it's having a loving partner, a job, good health, enough to eat, or simply being able to appreciate a beautiful sunset. If you're struggling with negativity, take the time to think about things you are grateful for.

Meditation. Meditation doesn't just help you to find calm and focus, it can also be used specifically to boost positivity and gratitude. Use meditation to break out of a negative cycle.

Exercise and diet. Eating and drinking too much of the wrong stuff and not getting enough exercise can leave you feeling sluggish and negative. Eating healthy stuff and getting exercise do the opposite. You know what you need to do...

Self-care. Too much stress can make you feel negative. You need to allow time for relaxation and fun in order to stay positive.

For me, the realization that I wasn't just a helpless participant in my thoughts, but that I was able to control and direct them, was possibly the most important discovery I have ever made. You don't just look at the world and see what's out there. Your brain creates a story in which you participate. It can be a horror story, filled with fear and threats. Or it can be a success story about seeing opportunity and potential for improvement. You get to choose which story you play a part in.

With all the distractions of the modern world and the constant stream of information to which we are continually subjected, it can be difficult to focus on being positive. Fortunately, there is a great technique that can help you to find calm during the most hectic day. That's what we'll be talking about in the next Chapter.

CHILL

How To Create A Mental Environment For Confidence

Do not ruin today with mourning tomorrow.

– Catherynne M. Valente

I want you to learn to meditate. *It will truly change your life*

You'd be amazed at how many people have strange ideas about what meditation is and what it does. Some are deeply suspicious. Surely meditation is just for hippies and wimps? It's not, you know. Meditation is easy to do, simple and it brings immediate and concrete benefits.

Buddhist teaching includes a lot of useful stuff, but one of the ideas that most appeals to me is called *"monkey mind."* The analogy describes a mind that is constantly, relentlessly moving from thought to thought, like a monkey swinging rapidly from one branch to another. It's about a chaotic stream of rapidly changing thoughts that move from one to the other without ever giving you the chance to achieve anything. Have you ever laid down in bed at night and, instead of drifting off to sleep, you find yourself endlessly thinking about what you have done (or not done) in the past and what you need to do in the future? Have you ever been faced by having lots of things that need to be done, but you just can't get started because your brain races from one to another, screaming about how urgent they all are? That's monkey mind. Psychologists often refer to it as *overthinking*, but I rather like the Buddhist name.

Meditation is a fantastic way of dealing with monkey mind. Here's how you do it:

- Find a quiet place where you won't be disturbed or interrupted.
- Find a comfortable position. You can stand, sit or even lie down. It doesn't matter, provided that you won't be distracted by the need to fidget or change position.

- Close your eyes and relax.
- You'll most likely find that those racing thoughts continue, so you're going to focus on your breathing. Count each time you inhale and exhale. Or you can use a traditional Buddhist technique where you visualize a swinging door. Each time you inhale, you visualize it swinging one way. As you exhale you visualize it swinging the other way.

That's it. See, I told you it was simple! How long should you keep this up? Five minutes is probably a good place to start. How often should you do it? Once every day is good, but three or four times a week is OK as long as you do it regularly. As you get more experienced, you may want to try it more often and for longer. When you start out, you'll probably find that those racing thoughts continue. Just stay with it and focus on your breathing. They will gradually slow and still.

I know that it probably doesn't sound like much, but meditating like this can help to calm your mind and leave you feeling refreshed and energized. Respected studies suggest that it does a whole collection of other things too. It can increase the size of the parts of your brain used for learning and memory[29]. It can be as effective as drugs in fighting depression[30]. It can dramatically reduce activity in the default mode network (DMN), the part of your brain responsible for overthinking[31].

Even better, as little as two weeks of regular meditation can bring about measurable improvements[32]. Many people report significant improvements somewhere between two weeks and one month after starting meditation. And even better still, meditation makes it much easier to access another concept that originally comes from Buddhist teaching: mindfulness.

That's probably something else you may have heard of. However, just as with meditation there are a great many misconceptions about just what this is. It's a complex topic and whole books have been written about mindfulness, but here's the short version: mindfulness means learning to be in the present moment, giving your entire attention to what you're doing right now. That probably doesn't sound terribly impressive, but just think about it for a moment.

You spend more time than is useful thinking about the future and the past. You have negative feelings of guilt and regret for past actions and you worry about what may happen in the future. The problem is that these are completely useless thoughts that represent wasted effort. You can't change the past. You can't control the future. If instead you can give your whole attention and maximum effort to what you're doing right now, the future will take care of itself and you'll be able to see the past in its proper context.

Just like meditation, mindfulness is simple. Your brain is an awesome machine, capable of changing the world. But you waste its power by allowing racing thoughts of the past and the future to dominate your thinking. If you could harness all of your brain's abilities to focus on the present moment, you could achieve so much more. That's why mindfulness is so powerful. Many very successful sports stars currently use mindfulness to improve their performance. Business executives also increasingly use this technique to improve their ability to focus. But how can you develop mindfulness?

Meditation is a good starting point. Because it helps to still your racing thoughts, meditation inherently makes you focus on the present moment. Even after you have finished meditating, that ability spills over into what follows. But you don't just find mindfulness through meditation. You can make almost any activity mindful.

Let's suppose you are walking. Maybe you're on your way to work, perhaps you're between meetings or you might just be taking a pleasant Sunday morning stroll in the countryside. Most people only give a little of their attention to what they're experiencing while they walk. They're thinking about what they're going to do when they arrive, about that movie they watched last night or they're listening to music or a podcast.

Being mindful means forgetting about the music and the podcast and making a conscious effort to immerse yourself in the messages your senses bring. Listen to the sound of your footsteps, the wind in the trees or even the sound of traffic at a busy intersection. Really look at what's around you. There is always something interesting to see if you take the time to notice it. Feel what your feet are doing: are they crunching through leaves, slopping through mud or just slapping rhythmically on tarmac? Make a conscious effort to completely immerse yourself in the experience. You'll discover that there is a whole Surround-sound, 3D, Technicolor world out there. And by learning to appreciate that, you're training your brain to become mindful.

You can be mindful in absolutely anything. Next time you are washing the car, really feel the shiny paint, smell the cleaning liquid, see how shiny that chrome is. Give any activity 100% of your attention, drink in the information from your senses and consciously avoid thoughts of what has come before or may come next and you will be mindful.

To achieve anything worthwhile you need focus. The more intense the focus, the more effective you'll be. Monkey mind blocks focus. Meditation and mindfulness fight monkey mind and improve focus. So, what are you waiting for?

One of the things that you will have become more aware of through reading this book is how much the people around you affect how you feel about yourself. Positive people make you feel respected, valued, supported, and loved. They make you feel more self-confident. Negative people do the precise opposite. But there is a very important question you need to ask yourself: are you one of the positive people? That's what we'll be talking about in the next Chapter.

22

PASS IT ON

How To Create A Life Of Escalating Confidence

Having friends who are accepting, supportive, available, and loving are key to feeling safe. If you choose to cultivate better friendships, begin by being a great friend to others.

– Tara Bianca

When was the last time you gave someone a compliment for no other reason that you thought it would make them feel good? When was the last time you told someone how great they are and how much you respect, love and admire them? When was the last time you reached out to someone to give them support?

Be honest here. If you're like many people, you're probably so wrapped-up in thinking about yourself that you may often forget to do these things. If you're a man, it may be even harder. We guys can find things like emotions hard to deal with and even harder to express. I have been with my wife for over thirty years. She's probably the smartest, prettiest, hardest-working person I know and she somehow manages to combine that with genuine care and affection for other people. But in the past, I used to go for way too long without telling her how much I admire and love her. That wasn't good. Obviously, it wasn't good for her but also for me. I learned that I needed to change, that I needed to make a conscious effort to express my positive feelings for her. You need to learn that too.

When you see someone else succeed, or behave in a way that you admire, or try out a new look that suits them, it's perfectly normal to feel an initial brief twinge of jealousy or even envy. But you need to temper that by thinking about two things: first, don't compare yourself to other people. If someone else does something admirable, don't allow that to make you feel diminished because you haven't done the same. Use it to inspire you to achieve your own version of greatness.

Second, some people seem to have an in-built feeling that there is only so much success to go around. That's partly because we are taught, directly and indirectly, that life is inherently competitive. If that was true, then the only way to succeed would be to compete harder to grab more of that limited stock of success from others. Objectively, that's stupid. Co-operation and support will beat competition, every time. The only measure of success that truly matters is the progress you are making towards achieving your goals. If someone else succeeds, that doesn't leave less success for you. Celebrate their success just as you would your own. Because soon, you'll be succeeding too. Most of all, take the time to let other people know how great you think they are.

Notice when someone has achieved something or done something well. Or if someone has made a bold choice or overcome a problem or simply if they're looking great. Make the effort to tell them that you have noticed and that you recognize what they have done. Praise them. Think about how good praise and recognition feel to you. They feel just as good to other people. When you make a conscious effort to do this, you'll notice something amazing happening: other people will start to do the same for you.

I spent part of my working life running a large business. When I arrived to take the post of General Manager, productivity was OK and the company was making a regular, though not spectacular, profit. The people who hired me just seemed to want more of the same. After a couple of weeks in the role, I wasn't so sure.

One of the things that I noticed was that my predecessor had encouraged different departments (and even people within departments) to compete with one another. Reports were posted in the dining area where the relative performance of each department was highlighted. Reading the minutes of previous meetings showed that my predecessor had emphasized these to department heads. Each department was encouraged to out-perform the others. But the company was missing out on something really important: unified teamwork. The separate departments were performing well separately but they just weren't pulling together.

I changed that. The comparison of performance between departments went. In its place came performance information for the company as a whole. I made a conscious effort to praise effort wherever I saw it. I consciously did not make comparisons between people or departments. It took around three months for that ethos to embed. When it did, the change was significant. Departments began to work together for the first time. Procurement introduced a streamlined ordering system that allowed us to reduce stock. But that took extra resources and the benefits only showed up in the bottom line of the stock department. Previously, procurement might not have done that because it would have boosted what they saw as a competitor. After six months in the role, I saw a building ethos of support and encouragement that made that office a much more pleasant place to work. That was, not coincidentally, accompanied by increased turnover and profitability.

You can make the same change in your life, not just in your work but in your personal relationships too. On your own, there is only so much that you can achieve. As part of a supportive network of people working together, you can do much better. You can also significantly reduce your levels of stress. You can instigate that change by making the effort to give praise and encouragement, not indiscriminately, but where they're due. You'll find that doing this helps to build a network of encouraging and supportive people around you. That increases your self-confidence and allows you to achieve more than you might have thought possible.

This also applies to the support you can find in places like the LearnWell Community.

Of course, the opposite is true too. If you are critical, other people will be critical of you. If you're unsupportive, people will not support you. If you never give praise, you won't get it back. This is a choice you make. If you want to be supported, encouraged and valued, begin by showing other people how much you support, encourage and value them. It really is that simple. You make a choice as to whether you are a positive friend, partner and colleague. That choice defines whether you spend life surrounded by positive people.

Go and tell someone how great they are. Right now. ♥

PART 4

Your Confidence In Action

Now, you know everything you need to know. You have all the information required. It's time for you to take that information and to translate it into practical action. It's time for you to start walking the walk. To help you do this, I want to share with you some stories about people who have managed to make real changes to their lives through building their self-confidence.

Names and some details have been changed. Otherwise, these stories are recounted as they happened. Each scenario looks at different circumstances and each person involved uses different techniques. Each examines a particular situation that presents challenges for a person and their self-confidence. All of these are covered in this book: it's through my own experience and by observing people and situations like these that I have created the approach detailed here.

I hope you'll find these scenarios inspirational. It's easy to forget that other people lack self-confidence too. By using the right approach and restoring their self-confidence step-by-step, many of them have overcome this problem. Mike, Sue, Anne, Pete and Sonia will show you how. Using the guidance in this book, you can do the same.

SCENARIO 1: MIKE WALKING INTO A ROOM

Mike paused outside the door for a moment, listening to the muted murmur of conversation inside. He took a deep breath. He was still a little nervous, but for the first time he was actually looking forward to this. It was just a quick, casual get-to-know-you social event with drinks and a few nibbles. His boss had pointed out that the new clients would be there and that it was a great way to make new contacts. A couple of hours, tops. No big issue, right?

In the past, Mike had dreaded this kind of social event. Talking about work was fine, but just chatting to people had always made him feel nervous. What should he talk about? What if people didn't like him? Was this shirt OK for a work social event? Would anyone notice if he left after half an hour or so? Those worries had made him avoid social events. His boss had even mentioned it at his last appraisal: "*Just make a little more effort. Get to know people. No biggie, but it would make a difference.*"

Now, armed with his new knowledge, he was ready to try out a fresh approach. In the past, he would have slunk in the door, avoided eye-contact, made his way to the drinks table and then found a quiet corner where he could hide. Instead, he made a conscious effort to straighten his shoulders, push open the door and stride confidently in. He had learned that just looking confident affected how people reacted to him.

He deliberately looked round the room, making eye-contact with the people he knew and smiling at them. He still had to make himself do this, but he knew that it made a positive difference to how people saw him. He got a drink and then walked over to where Tom, his boss, was chatting to three of the new clients, two men and a woman. He was introduced and started asking them questions, not about work but about themselves: did they have a good trip? What did they think of the city? Was it different to where they lived?

He made a conscious effort to really listen to their replies. He knew that in the past, he had been so concerned with what people thought of him (or with wondering how soon he could leave) that he really hadn't paid much attention. Now, he listened carefully and asked follow-on questions. The woman didn't have much to say at first. He could tell by the way that she constantly smoothed her hair and kept looking around that she was feeling nervous. She asked him questions, but then clearly didn't listen to his responses.

In the past, he might have put that down to the fact that he simply wasn't very interesting. Now, he understood that it was simply the woman's response to feeling uncomfortable. Realizing that other people also felt unconfident and unsure of themselves was probably the most important discovery that Mike made. Once he learned to see the signs of discomfort in other people, that made him feel less like the odd man out and more able to empathize and communicate with them in a meaningful way.

He continued chatting with the woman, even though she was still clearly distracted. Then, he mentioned music, and suddenly he had her full attention. She became animated and interested when it became apparent that they both enjoyed the same artists.

It was only while laughing when she described a particularly terrible concert she had attended that Mike suddenly realized: he was having fun …

If you lack self-confidence, simply walking into a room, particularly one that includes people you don't know, can seem incredibly daunting. It's something that's very difficult for confident people to understand. Mike used to feel that way but he has learned how to overcome his nervousness. I want you to think about what's going on here in terms of the guidance in this book. I'll provide Chapter references: feel free to go back and reread the text and think about how it applies to Mike's situation.

First of all, and like many people who lack confidence, in the past Mike was completely self-absorbed. When he stepped into that room, he was convinced that everyone was looking at him. When he spoke, he felt that people were carefully weighing what he said and judging that too. Mike has learned to see that he isn't the most important person in that room and certainly not the only one feeling nervous and unconfident (Chapter 6).

Mike has also learned that other people in the room are projecting an image that is not necessarily true. That woman he chats to might seem aloof or even arrogant, but Mike can now see that she is probably just feeling awkward and isolated (Chapter 5). He has also learned that people react more positively to him if he can project a confident image. They don't know how he used to be: they only see how he is now, and if that's confident and assured, that's how they assume he is.

In the past, Mike just didn't listen. He was so busy wondering what others were thinking of him that he didn't give them any of his full attention. That didn't make people want to talk to him. In fact, it made them avoid talking to him and that further undermined his confidence. Now, Mike has learned to be mindful, fully engaged in the present moment. He uses meditation to help him do this but he also makes a conscious effort to give all his attention not to racing thoughts inside his head but to what is actually happening around him and what people are saying (Chapter 21).

Mike still finds that attending social events makes him feel a little uncomfortable. However, he has come to accept this and to understand that the more he does it, the less uncomfortable he feels (Chapter 7). Now, he has reached the point where he actually finds talking to new people fun (Chapter 10). Instead of dreading social events, he rather looks forward to them. Each time he attends one and has a good time, he looks forward to them a little more. That places him firmly on an ascending confidence cycle (Chapter 3).

Mike has come to learn where his lack of confidence comes from. He was badly bullied at school which meant that he performed badly in several subjects though he is intelligent and a quick learner. He learned that doing well in class just focused the attention of the bullies on him and instead, he pretended to be as dumb as them. His father (a supremely confident and rather overbearing man) expected great things of him and couldn't understand why his reports and exam results weren't as good as they should have been. Failing to gain his father's approval further diminished Mike's confidence. Coming to understand this has helped Mike to clearly see where his lack of confidence comes from, making him better able to deal with it (Chapter 2).

Mike was so unconfident that he found attending any social event traumatic. He still feels a little nervous (and that's perfectly normal), but that gets less every time he does it. And when he discovers that he's having fun while socializing, he is clearly on the road to enhanced confidence.

SCENARIO 2: SUE GOING FOR A JOB INTERVIEW

Sue was preparing for a job interview and, for the first time that she could remember, she wasn't absolutely terrified by the prospect. She had always found any kind of interview an ordeal. In the past, job interviews had been such a frightening prospect that on occasion, she hadn't applied for a position simply because she couldn't face the idea of the interview.

She knew that was stupid. She wasn't happy in her present job: it paid the bills but it was rather dull and didn't give her many opportunities to use her skills. Now, sitting and waiting to be called for the interview, she felt calm. She even felt, she was surprised to discover, eager to go in and start the interview. That made her think about just how she had managed to develop this new, positive approach?

Probably the single most important thing was coming to identify her strengths. That wasn't something she had thought about before. She had simply muddled along from day to day, doing her best to deal with the demands of her current job. It was only when she sat back and thought about it that she realized that one of her main strengths was her ability to communicate with and encourage other people. People often came to her when they had a problem and she seemed to be able to make them feel better and to suggest things they could do. In her present job, she had little chance to use those skills, which was why she hadn't really thought about their importance. Now, she had decided to apply for a management position where she felt those abilities would really help.

Understanding what she was really good at made her feel much more confident about the interview. She <u>knew</u> she'd be good at this job, and knowing that made her feel quite different. Instead of dreading the questions she might be asked, she looked forward to explaining why she felt suited to this job. She had also come to the realization that comparing herself to other people wasn't a good way to prepare for an interview. If she did that, it seemed that perhaps there were lots of other people who would be better qualified and better able to do the job. However, on looking around, she soon began to see that the image of confidence and capability that many people project wasn't real.

One of the most important things she had learned was not to listen to what people say, but to watch what they do. Her own line manager appeared extremely confident. However, when she really looked at how he behaved, she could see that he lacked empathy and understanding. When she examined certain situations in detail, she was amazed to see that she could actually have handled them better. That gave her confidence a giant boost, but it also made her begin to think about how important the image we project is.

People like confidence. In a situation such as a job interview, confidence suggests your belief that you can do the job. That's a major plus point for any interviewer. After all, if someone doesn't seem to believe that they can do the job, why should an interviewer think any differently? While she was waiting, Sue repeated positive affirmations to herself, helping her to avoid overthinking and get into a positive state of mind. When she was finally called into the interview room, she made a conscious and determined effort to stand, straight, walk confidently, make eye-contact with the interviewers and to sit in a relaxed way and not to fidget. On the inside, she still felt a little nervous, but she knew that being able to radiate confidence was a vital part of getting any job.

One of the things that had helped her to relax was her new willingness to consider what would happen if she didn't get the job. No matter how well qualified she was or how well she did in the interview, there was always the chance that she wouldn't succeed. Before, she had found the idea of rejection terrifying. Now, she had learned to reduce her fear of failure and even to accept that, if she didn't get this job, that wasn't the end of the story. There were always other jobs to apply for and if she learned something from each interview, she'd get one of those even if she didn't get this one. She sat back, smiled and prepared to answer the interviewer's questions...

I don't know if Sue gets this job or not, but I do know that her approach is exactly right. Job interviews are never easy. They are always a challenge but they are something that many of us will face. However, your chances are substantially reduced if you approach them without confidence. What are the important things that Sue has learned?

First and most importantly, she has learned to really understand what her strengths are (Chapter 4). I can't emphasize how important this is. When you lack confidence, it's easy to slip into a state of mind that tells you that you're lousy at everything. That simply isn't true. Your experience, knowledge and personality mean that there are things that you're really good at. You just need to take the time to ensure that you know what those are. Sue hadn't really thought about her people skills at all, she just took them for granted as something she was innately good at. It took her time to see that they could be used to advantage in a management position. When you're going for an interview, knowing that the job will allow you to use your strengths should give your confidence a major boost and will mean that you don't suffer from Imposter Syndrome (Chapter 2). And if the job won't allow you to use your strengths, maybe it's the wrong job for you?

If you're going for an interview, you will be compared to the other people being interviewed. That's inevitable, but don't be tempted to compare yourself to others. Doing that can only undermine your confidence and we know that the image that other people present can be false (Chapter 5) so you may be comparing yourself to a fantasy. Now that you know how to recognize the signs of a lack of confidence in other people (Chapter 6), also make sure you aren't giving those signs to your interviewers. Think about your body-language, make eye-contact and try to smile and relax.

Affirmations (Chapter 15) are a great way to prepare for an interview (or any other potentially stressful situation). When you're traveling to the interview or waiting your turn, repeat positive affirmations inside your head. These will give you a great positive mental boost that will help to put you in a confident state of mind. Practice mindfulness (Chapter 21) during the interview. Don't allow yourself to be distracted by thoughts about what you have done in the past or worries about the future. Be absolutely in the moment and give your entire attention to what's happening in the interview.

You know that taking action is the most important thing you can do (Chapter 8). You can think all you want, but until you translate that thought into action, nothing will change. Going for a job interview is taking action. By doing that, you will make progress whether you get the job or not. You will learn from the experience. If you take that learning on-board, you are moving forward. The only failure that ultimately matters isn't failing to get the job but allowing your lack of confidence to prevent you from taking the interview.

SCENARIO 3: ANNE LEARNING TO ASSERT HERSELF

Someone once referred to Anne as *"just a girl who can't say no."* It seemed to have been said as a joke. Other people present certainly smiled, but it troubled her. She went home and looked it up and discovered that it was a reference to a line from a song in a 1950s musical movie. She listened to the lyrics:

*"I'm just a girl who can't say no,
I'm in a terrible fix,
I always say 'come on, let's go'
Just when I ought to say nix."*

It was kind of a fun song and it echoed round inside her head irritatingly for several days. But was that really how people saw her? As someone who couldn't assert herself, a pushover who couldn't say "*no*" in any circumstances? Initially, she was angry. How dare someone suggest that about her! Then, she started to think about it. When was the last time she had said no to someone who asked for something? When was the last time she had spoken up and asserted her own opinion and explained her own needs? She was embarrassed and a little astonished to discover that she couldn't remember a single instance. Were they right, was she a girl who just couldn't say no?

She thought about it again a few days later. She was having lunch with a friend. That didn't happen often and it almost always meant that the friend wanted her to look after Moppet, her cat. Her friend often went away for weekends or longer, and when she did, Anne always looked after the cat. It had become a habit but the truth was that Anne didn't like cats in general and especially not Moppet, a large, spoiled Abyssinian with a piercing cry.

Moppet came with a litter tray which Anne hated cleaning out. He also sharpened his claws on the front of her sofa, despite also being provided with an expensive cat-gym which he never used. At night, he cried constantly: he was used to sleeping on his owner's bed and couldn't understand why Anne didn't allow him to do the same. When she actually thought about it, Anne dreaded looking after Moppet. So, how come she found herself doing that several times a year?

It wasn't as though Moppet's owner was even a particularly close friend. In fact, the only time this person showed any interest in seeing her was when she needed some free cat-sitting. Anne went to lunch fully intending to say no to looking after the cat. Somehow, that wasn't how it worked out. Instead of immediately agreeing, she made some vague comments about how busy she was and mentioned that she had recently bought a new sofa, hoping the friend would take the hint. She didn't. Instead, she seemed to assume that Anne would be happy to look after Moppet as usual. That evening, as Anne sat with a glass of wine gloomily watching Moppet shred the front of her new sofa, she made a promise to herself: she wasn't going to be the girl who couldn't say "*no*" anymore!

She got her first opportunity just a few weeks later. Same friend, same lunch, same request for cat-sitting services. Anne said "*No, I can't.*" She had to bite her tongue not to apologize or offer invented excuses, but she managed to let her refusal hang in the air. Initially, the friend was disconcerted. She asked why? Anne explained about the litter tray, the sofa and the crying that kept her awake. The friend became irritated. Anne had always looked after Moppet before. That meant that she'd have to take him to a cattery, which he hated. Anne simply explained that she wouldn't be looking after Moppet again. The lunch became a little frosty.

Afterwards, Anne was amazed at how empowered and energized she felt. Saying "*no*" hadn't been easy, but now she felt really good. That evening, as she looked around her cat-free apartment, she couldn't help but smile. She had a feeling that she might not be receiving a lunch invitation from that friend anytime soon. But do you know what? That didn't trouble her nearly as much as she had anticipated. That friend hadn't really been interested in her, hadn't really asked much about what she was doing and in retrospect, had wanted only to find a holiday home for Moppet. If that friend no longer wanted to see her, well, maybe that was someone her life might be better without?

Dealing with the Moppet situation also made her think more about how good asserting herself by saying no had made her feel. It had made her feel in control and more confident. Maybe that was something she needed to do more of? She had a big progress meeting coming up at work. Anne was in charge of a small team working on a large project. The team were already working at full-stretch, but she knew that she was likely to be asked to take on additional work at the meeting.

One of the other teams had fallen behind. The Project Manager had already hinted that she'd be asked to take on some of the work of the other team. She was dreading the meeting. She knew how disheartened the members of her own team would be if she agreed to more work, but she couldn't refuse. Could she?

She prepared for the meeting and actually wrote down what she planned to say:

> *If I take on this extra work, the members of my team will be stressed and less effective because they are already working at full capacity.*

She resisted the temptation to put the word "*sorry*" in there somewhere, or to offer excuses. She hated speaking up in front of a group, but writing this down in advance made her feel more confident. She went to the meeting. She was asked to take on the additional work. She made her statement and then waited. There was a brief silence. Then, the Project Manager simply said that perhaps they'd have to find other ways of dealing with the situation and the meeting moved smoothly on.

Anne was stunned. It had worked! She had said what she felt, stood up for her team and wow, it felt good! Even more surprisingly, none of her colleagues seemed to think any less of her and the members of her own team were delighted with what she had done. Even the Project Manager seemed to approve and later, privately, told her that it was probably for the best. Perhaps she was becoming a girl who could say "*no*"...

Are you a girl (or boy) who just can't say no? Many of us are. We feel that saying no will make people like us less. The truth is that isn't generally so and where it is, well perhaps those aren't people we want to spend time with?

The truth is that not everyone is going to like you (Chapter 9). You do need to accept that and as your self-confidence grows, you'll find that easier to do. It isn't a reflection of your worth as a person. You must also recognize that not all relationships are equal. Some people will give you support and encouragement. They will want to spend time with you for the sheer pleasure of it. Cherish those relationships. Some people are needy, some are users, just like Moppet's owner. They're in a relationship with you because of what they can get out of it. If saying "*no*" to those people means that they want to spend less time with you, perhaps that isn't such a bad thing?

You have boundaries, personal, emotional and physical (Chapter 18). They matter. If you allow those to be regularly ignored, you're going to feel bad about yourself and negative towards the people crossing those boundaries. That's why Anne ends up not just angry and irritated when Moppet visits, but also disappointed with herself. You do have to think about where your boundaries lie, to tell people about them and to be prepared to enforce them by asserting yourself.

Learning to assert yourself (Chapter 17) is a vital skill. You have a right to say how you feel and what you need. You have an absolute right to say "*no.*" We say "*yes*" to something when we aren't really keen, and then we find it even more difficult to refuse the same request a second time. Then, we can find ourselves doing things we really don't want to and that makes us feel resentful and undermines our self-confidence. Just like Anne, you can use three-part assertion messages to explain how you feel about any situation. Just doing that will make you feel better and should lead to a resolution of the issue.

Learning to assert yourself and to say "*no*" aren't easy. But if you take a deep breath and use the techniques in this book, you will find that you can do it. And just like Anne, you'll be amazed at how empowered and confident doing those things will make you feel.

SCENARIO 4: PETE GOING ON A BLIND DATE

Pete was going on a blind date and he was looking forward to it! Six months ago, he wouldn't have believed that was possible. He had gone through a divorce three years ago. In truth, it hadn't been too traumatic: both he and his wife June had come to realize that it just wasn't working out, though it was she who had first raised the issue of splitting up. There hadn't been anyone else involved (as far as he knew) and he remained on fairly good terms with his ex-wife.

He had found himself in his mid-thirties and, for the first time since he was a teenager, on his own and free to make his own choices. In retrospect, he could see that he hadn't coped well. He seemed to have drifted through the actual process of the divorce on autopilot. Even when it was finalized and he and June were living separately, somewhere inside his head, he still assumed that they'd get back together at some point. When he thought about the future, it was still in terms of the dreams and aspirations that he had shared with his wife.

He started dating fairly quickly. The first few dates didn't go well. It was only looking back on them later that he saw that he was (usually unconsciously) comparing each date to June. Worse still, he was still so wrapped-up in his own hurt and confusion that he didn't really pay any attention to those women or what they had to say. It took an emotional scene with June where she made it clear that, whatever her future held, it didn't include him, before he was finally forced to accept that his life was going to be very different.

He'd gone through a bad time for a few months. It wasn't until a friend sat him down and talked to him that he began to see light at the end of the tunnel. The friend explained that while losing June was obviously painful, it wasn't all bad. Yes, that part of his life was over, but that meant that he could choose what the rest of his life would look like. Initially, he hadn't been able to accept that. But then he began to see that it was true: the future was his to choose. With that simple switch of perception, the future shimmered with countless potential opportunities.

The breakthrough didn't come all at once, but rather as a series of mini-revelations. He did want to be in a relationship. If he gave up on dating, that wouldn't happen. He wanted to spend time with someone supportive and interested, someone who really listened to what he had to say. But he didn't behave that way. He began to use a simple guide to assess his own behavior: would I want to be with someone who acted as I do? Suddenly, what to do on dates seemed clear.

He went on several more dates, and they were much better. None of the women he dated were "*the one*," but he had fun and he hoped that they had too. And as he grew used to acting with compassion and empathy and thinking about the other person, a strange thing happened: he found that he liked himself better. Instead of subconsciously wondering why the Hell anyone would want to spend time with him, he started to see himself as a fun companion. Each date might not be the start of a life-long relationship but hey, as long as they both had a good time, that was enough.

And now, a well-meaning friend had set him up with a blind date. All he knew was that she was a teacher in her mid-thirties, divorced and like him, without children. He was excited at the idea of meeting with a complete stranger. He was actually looking forward very much to this date. It would be fun! They'd both have a good time. Now, should he wear that fancy new shirt...

Dating can be challenging if you lack confidence. The idea of a blind date might seem completely terrifying. But just like Pete, you can learn not just to dread this less, but to actually enjoy it.

Pete's journey towards confidence began with acceptance (Chapter 15). All the time that he still believed that he might have a future with June, he couldn't move on. June's final rejection of that idea might have been painful at the time, but it forced him to accept that his future would not feature her as his partner. Only when he had accepted that could he begin to heal and make progress.

Your perception of the world only exists inside your own head. Precisely the same situation can look positive or negative depending on how you perceive it (Chapter 20). Pete was seeing his break-up with June as negative, as the end of long-cherished dreams and hopes. It was only when he spoke with his friend that he began to perceive it quite differently, as an opportunity to rebuild his life in any way that he wanted. Same situation, different perception. That was another giant step for Pete.

Pete's next significant realization was that he needed to turn himself into the kind of person he'd want to spend time with (Chapter 22). He made a conscious effort to become genuinely interested in the women he met, in discovering their personalities, dreams and aspirations. He paid them compliments and made positive comments. That made him a better date but it also helped him to love himself (Chapter 19). If you don't love yourself, the chances of finding anyone else who will love you are slim.

As Pete got better at dating, he began to enjoy the process much more. He looked forward to meeting new women and finding out about them. He had positive expectations of each date (Chapter 3) and that helped him get onto an ascending confidence cycle. His enjoyment of the process of dating also helped him to manage his expectations. If the person he dated didn't turn out to be someone that he could spend the rest of his life with, well, that didn't make it a failure as long as both of them had a pleasant evening. Pete had learned to keep going (Chapter 16). Each date might not be with a person with whom he would have an immediate and deep connection. But who knows what the next date would bring? Pete realized that the only failure that would really matter would be if he stopped dating altogether.

SCENARIO 5: SONIA STARTING HER OWN BUSINESS

When Sonia was made redundant, it had briefly seemed like the end of the world. She hadn't especially loved her job or found it particularly fulfilling, but after working for the same company for over fifteen years, the prospect of not having that job had seemed terrifying. The company had given her a generous redundancy package, so money wasn't an immediate problem. That gave her some time to think.

Deciding what to do was a problem. At first, she had started looking for another job. She didn't see anything that she was qualified and experienced for or anything that looked enticing. However, she also remembered something that a friend had once said to her: *"The Chinese symbol for "crisis" is made up of two characters, one for "danger" and the other for "opportunity"."* Sonia had looked it up later and discovered that this wasn't actually true, but the notion that sudden, unexpected change also brought opportunity had stuck with her. Losing her job surely felt like a crisis, but perhaps it was also an opportunity?

Sonia had always loved ceramics. At school she had first discovered the pleasure of shaping clay on a wheel and then firing and painting it to create a tiny work of art. She discovered that she was good at it too, and when she found herself living in an apartment with a spare bedroom, it didn't take long for her to equip it as a ceramics workshop. Over weekends and evenings, she lost herself in the sensual pleasure of creating new pieces. Her home quickly became cluttered with beautiful items, and she began giving them away to friends. To her surprise, they seemed delighted. They even began asking when she might be making new pieces? More than one suggested that she should try selling them.

The redundancy meant that she suddenly found herself with a great deal of spare time. She spent a lot of it in her workshop. Gradually, and she couldn't remember when precisely the idea had taken hold, she began to wonder whether instead of looking for another job, she could start her own business making and selling ceramics?

Initially, that felt like a daunting prospect. She had no idea of how to start or run a business. She began by drawing up a list of questions: would she need a permit to run a business from her home, how would she declare and pay taxes, how could she sell the pieces she made? She researched these online, and found that many of the answers were easy to find and not as complicated as she had feared. A friend recommended an accountant and she had met with him to discuss what she planned to do. He had given useful advice and seemed always to be happy to answer her many questions.

He also advised her to draw up a business plan. She didn't need a loan to start the business, but he explained that drawing up a detailed plan would allow her to understand what she would need to achieve in terms of sales to break-even. He also explained that this would help her to set a date by which she either needed the business to be viable or she'd have to consider taking another job.

She took his advice. The money from her redundancy package would last nine months, if she was careful. She'd give herself six months of running her own business and then make a decision about whether she could continue. The accountant helped her to file the paperwork she needed to start the business and register it for the necessary taxes. She paid a young web designer who created a wonderful web site which would be her main means of generating sales. She also contacted a number of local craft shops who agreed to take some of her products on a "*sale or return*" basis.

Now, here she was, with her finger poised over the keyboard, ready to click the key that would finally launch Merriweather Ceramics. She was so excited…

Launching your own business is a big thing. It can seem complicated and frighteningly uncertain, but Sonia is going about it in precisely the right way.

First and most importantly, the business is based on something she already knows she's good at, that she's passionate about and that she loves doing. In any enterprise, playing to your strengths (Chapter 4) exponentially increases your chances of success. Sonia already has all the equipment and supplies she needs to get started, and that's also an important success factor (Chapter 8). Significantly, by planning to start her own business, Sonia has also changed her perception of her redundancy from a threat to an opportunity (Chapter 20). Her situation hasn't changed but the way that she sees it has. That allows her to make the best of her circumstances.

Starting a ceramics business is a big thing (Chapter 13). It's inspirational, it's something that Sonia passionately wants to succeed. It's something worth devoting all her energy to. However, getting to the point that she's ready to launch means doing a series of small things first (Chapter 12). What can seem like a daunting task, like starting your own business, can actually be broken down into a series of smaller and more easily achievable steps. Sonia's on-line research, asking advice from the accountant and employing a professional web designer have all helped her to complete these smaller steps and now she's ready for the big step of starting the business. Taking these small steps also helps to get Sonia used to the idea of taking action (Chapter 12). She isn't just thinking about starting a business now: she's taking concrete steps to make it happen. And every time she completes one of these smaller steps or overcomes a potential problem, her confidence increases.

Drawing up a business plan is a great idea. Fear, especially fear of the unknown, blocks people from taking action. By looking in detail at how the business needs to operate, and in considering what she'll do if it doesn't work out, Sonia is reducing that fear (Chapter 8). Setting a date when she'll decide whether the business is viable or not is also a great idea. This will allow Sonia to consider Smart Quitting (Chapter 16) if things don't work out. She knows that at that point, she'll still have enough money to keep her afloat while she looks for another job. This further reduces fear and uncertainty and increases her confidence.

By using the right techniques and approaches to build her confidence, Sonia is able to make a potentially life-changing choice that she would probably never have considered if it hadn't been for her redundancy. She can't fail. If the business prospers, she wins. If it doesn't, she has done something she loves for six months and she has learned a great deal that she may decide to put to use in the future. Either way, she will emerge from this process a more complete and confident person.

You can do the same.

IN 90 SECONDS YOU CAN MAKE A HUGE DIFFERENCE

If you feel we've deserved it, please take a moment to leave a review on Amazon.

Your feedback means the world to us. It helps us to improve and it means better learning experiences for all our readers.

We'd be so grateful to you for your review!

SUMMARY

You have reached the end: congratulations! I hope that you have learned a great deal as you worked your way through this book. But as we have already mentioned, this isn't a book about thinking, it's a book about doing. It's about taking what you have learned and translating that into practical changes to your everyday life.

I'd like you to think about that, to consider how you can apply what you have learned here to boost your self-confidence and transform your life. To help you visualize what that might look like, I want to show you a brief glimpse of the future, a snapshot of how a typical day may look once you apply these new techniques.

A DAY IN THE LIFE OF...

- You wake up but, before you get out of bed, you repeat your chosen affirmations because you know that these help to get you in a positive state of mind for the start of the day. You eat a healthy breakfast because you know that too helps to keep you feeling energized and positive.
- You set off for work, but you're going to try taking a different route. You know that taking the same old route every day is easy, but you find yourself operating on autopilot. So, you're trying as many different routes as you can. That prospect can initially make you feel uncomfortable, but every time you step outside the routine, it gets a little easier. You make a conscious effort to be mindful, to be fully engaged in the sights, sounds and experiences of your trip.

Summary

- You arrive at work feeling positive and keen to get started. You make the effort to smile and greet the people you meet, even those you don't know well. You know that how you present yourself makes a huge difference to how people perceive you: if you appear to be confident, people will assume that you are. Their belief increases your own self-confidence in an ascending cycle. You make an effort to pay at least one compliment to someone before you reach your desk. It doesn't matter what it is about: their appearance, something they have achieved at work, or something in their personal lives. You know what matters to the people you meet because you have taken the time to get to know them, to really listen to them. Giving out a *"well done"* makes them feel good, but it makes you feel good too.

- During the morning you and several of your colleagues must give a presentation to a potential new client. This was something you used to dread. However, when you spent time thinking about it, you realized that your anxiety about speaking in front of a group actually originated at school. You were often asked to give a reading at assembly. You were shy and self-effacing and you often stumbled over your words. As a result, you were mocked by some of your friends. Simply understanding where it comes from makes it easier to overcome that anxiety. You are also confident in your own knowledge and experience and in this meeting you will be playing to your strengths. However, when you arrive in the meeting room, you notice that some of your colleagues are looking very anxious. You know that they lack confidence so you make the effort to have a reassuring word with them.

- During the lunch break, you take the time to find a quiet place for a five minute meditation session. You have been doing this for some time and you know that this will leave you feeling refreshed and focused. You also take time out for gratitude: to think about at least three things for which you are grateful. This too has become part of your daily routine and you know that it leaves you in a positive state of mind.

- In the afternoon, you work on a large project you're involved in. This is about looking for new directions for the company, innovation that may lead to new opportunities. Some of your less confident colleagues don't want to get involved. They are worried by the fact that this is something entirely new and that it may fail. Those things don't worry you now. New and different is good and makes sure you step outside your comfort zone. And if it doesn't work out, well, you and the company will have learned a great deal that will help to make the correct future direction more obvious.

- When you leave the office, it's raining. In the past, you might have allowed this to make you feel miserable. Now, you take the time to smell the fresh wet grass and to notice the rainbow that's peeking over the adjacent building. You know that how you choose to perceive any situation affects how you feel. You choose to enjoy the rain and you arrive home feeling good.

- In the evening, you meet up with some friends to play badminton. They're a great bunch of people: positive and supportive and spending time with them always makes you feel happy. The competition is intense, but you don't feel miserable if you don't always win. You have learned not to compare yourself to others and instead to focus on your own performance. If you know that you have done your best and perhaps also improved a little, that's enough.

- Previously, you used to go to all sorts of social events, many of which you really didn't enjoy. It took you time to realize that you had a perfect right to say "*no.*" Asserting yourself in that way made you feel great and it made you think about the people you were spending time with. Some of those were people who were relentlessly negative. Some only spent time with you because they wanted something. You made a conscious effort not to spend time with them. Instead, you spend your time with people who are interested in you and you try to be supportive to and interested in them. Even better, you discover that spending time with these people is fun!

- You go back home, tired but content. You get into bed but, before you settle down for sleep, you review the day and assess how you have made progress towards your goals. One of your main goals is to increase your own self-confidence and you are happy to note that you have done several things during the day that will help to do that. Making progress feels good and you know that every time you do this, you create new neural pathways that help to make self-confidence a habit.

How does that compare to your typical day now? Wouldn't you rather have days filled with positivity that boost your self-confidence? Well, you can! If you use the techniques in this book, you can learn to become self-confident. It won't happen overnight, but it <u>will</u> happen.

You will have setbacks. You're human. Don't give up. Keep going. The guidance in this book really does work. It isn't magic, it simply involves the practical application of proven approaches. I truly believe that increasing your self-confidence is the single most significant change you can make in your life and that these approaches will allow you to do that.

So, what are you waiting for?

REFERENCES

1. *Confidence at work*, The University of Glasgow, 2017.
2. Elizabeth Hopper, *Maslow's Hierarchy of Needs Explained*, ThoughtCo, February 2020, retrieved from: https://www.thoughtco.com/maslows-hierarchy-of-needs-4582571
3. Roland Bénabou, Jean Tirole, *Self-Confidence and Personal Motivation*, Oxford Academic, The Quarterly Journal of Economics, August 2002.
4. Mark Murphy, *Neuroscience Explains Why You Need To Write Down Your Goals If You Actually Want To Achieve Them*, Forbes, April 2018, retrieved from: https://www.forbes.com/sites/markmurphy/2018/04/15/neuroscience-explains-why-you-need-to-write-down-your-goals-if-you-actually-want-to-achieve-them/
5. Gina Rippon, *The Gendered Brain: The New Neuroscience That Shatters The Myth Of The Female Brain,* The Bodley Head, 2019.
6. Caitlyn Collins, Professor of sociology at Washington University in St Louis, cited in: *The one word women need to be saying more often*, USA Today.
7. Michelle A. Harris, PhD, *The Link Between Self-Esteem and Social Relationships: A Meta-Analysis of Longitudinal Studies*, Journal of Personality and Social Psychology, September 2019.
8. Kruger, Justin, Dunning, David, *Unskilled and Unaware of It: How Difficulties in Recognizing One's Own Incompetence Lead to Inflated Self-Assessments*, Journal of Personality and Social Psychology, 1999.
9. Alberini CM, *Long-term memories: The good, the bad, and the ugly*, Cerebrum, 2010

10. Cacioppo JT, Cacioppo S, Gollan JK., *The negativity bias: Conceptualization, quantification, and individual differences*, Behavioral and Brain Sciences, 2014.

11. Nadia Goodman, *James Dyson on Using Failure to Drive Success*, Entrepreneur, November, 2012.

12. D. Watkins, *HBO doc shows how it's easy to make "Fake Famous" influencers, whose job is to "make you feel bad"*, Salon, February, 2021.

13. Arvind Hickman, *More than half of Instagram influencers engaged in fraud*, PR Week, April, 2021.

14. Daniela Tempesta, *Why You Should Stop Comparing Yourself to Others*, Huffington Post, February 2014.

15. Philip Jefferies, Michael Ungar, *Social anxiety in young people: A prevalence study in seven countries*, Plos One, September, 2020.

16. Olivia C. Bolt, Anke Ehlers, David M. Clark, *Faces in a Crowd: High Socially Anxious Individuals Estimate that More People Are Looking at Them than Low Socially Anxious Individuals*, Plos One, September, 2014.

17. Nico Bunzeck, Emrah Düzel, *Absolute Coding of Stimulus Novelty in the Human Substantia Nigra/VTA*, Neuron, June 2006.

18. Professor Saras D. Sarasvathy, *What Makes Entrepreneurs Entrepreneurial?*, University of Virginia, January 2008.

19. *US Military Seeks Sixth Sense Training*, LiveScience, March 2012.

20. Joel Pearson, *Measuring Intuition: Unconscious Emotional Information Boost Decision-Making Accuracy and Confidence*, Psychological Science, July 2014.

21. *Oxford English Dictionary* (O.E.D), 7th Edition, 2013.

22. Elizabeth Scott, PhD, *Why Having Fun Provides Some of the Best Stress Relief,* verywell mind, June 2020.
23. Marcel Schwantes, *6 Qualities of Extremely Likable People, According to Science*, Inc, retrieved from: https://www.inc.com/marcel-schwantes/science-says-these-6-traits-will-make-you-a-likabl.html
24. Kaiser Permanente, *Fun and friends help ease the pain of breast cancer*, ScienceDaily, May 2013.
25. Ruth Umoh, *Richard Branson: What 7 highly successful people can teach you about having fun while chasing your goals*, Make It, March 2018.
26. Claude M. Steele, *The Psychology of Self-Affirmation: Sustaining the Integrity of the Self*, Advances in Experimental Social Psychology, 1988.
27. J. David Creswell, Janine M. Dutcher, William M. P. Klein, Peter R. Harris, John M. Levine, *Self-Affirmation Improves Problem-Solving under Stress*, National Science Foundation, 2013.
28. Sam Kyle, *Hell Yeah or No: what's worth doing*, Hit Media 2020.
29. Brian Resnick, *"Reality" is constructed by your brain. Here's what that means, and why it matters*, Vox, June 2020.
30. Sara Lazar, Ph.D., *How Meditation Can Reshape Our Brains*, Harvard University, 2011.
31. Madhav Goyal, *Meditation Programs for Psychological Stress and Well-being: A Systematic Review and Meta-analysis*, JAMA Internal Medicine, 2014.
32. David McCormick, PhD, *New study finds links between meditation and brain functions*, Yale School of Medicine, 2012.

33. Michael D. Mrazek et al, *Mindfulness Training Improves Working Memory Capacity and GRE Performance While Reducing Mind Wandering*, Psychological Science, 2013

www.ingramcontent.com/pod-product-compliance
Lightning Source LLC
Chambersburg PA
CBHW061231070526
44584CB00030B/4072